International Conference on Recent Advances in Natural Language Processing (RANLP 2019)

Student Research Workshop

Varna, Bulgaria
2-4 September 2019

ISBN: 978-1-7138-0296-9

RANLPStud 2019

Proceedings of the
Student Research Workshop

associated with
**The 12th International Conference on
Recent Advances in Natural Language Processing
(RANLP 2019)**

2–4 September, 2019
Varna, Bulgaria

STUDENT RESEARCH WORKSHOP
ASSOCIATED WITH THE INTERNATIONAL CONFERENCE
RECENT ADVANCES IN
NATURAL LANGUAGE PROCESSING'2019

PROCEEDINGS

Varna, Bulgaria
2–4 September 2019

Series Online ISSN 2603-2821

Designed and Printed by INCOMA Ltd.
Shoumen, BULGARIA

Preface

The RANLP 2019 Student Research Workshop (RANLPStud 2019) is a special track of the established international conference Recent Advances in Natural Language Processing (RANLP 2019), now in its twelfth edition.

The RANLP Student Research Workshop is being organised for the sixth time and this year is running in parallel with the other tracks of the main RANLP 2019 conference. The target of RANLPStud 2019 is to be a discussion forum and provide an outstanding opportunity for students at all levels (Bachelor, Masters, and Ph.D.) to present their work in progress or completed projects to an international research audience and receive feedback from senior researchers.

The RANLP 2019 Student Research Workshop received a large number of submissions (23), a fact which was reflecting the record number of events, sponsors, submissions, and participants at the main RANLP 2019 conference.

We have accepted 2 excellent student papers as oral presentations and 12 submissions will be presented as posters. The final acceptance rate of the workshop was 60%.

We made our best to make the reviewing process in the best interest of our authors, by asking our reviewers to give as most exhaustive comments and suggestions as possible as well as to maintain an encouraging attitude. Each student submission was reviewed by 2 to 3 Programme Committee members, which are specialists in their field and were carefully selected to match the submission's topic.

This year, as usual, we invited both strictly Natural Language Processing (NLP) submissions, and submissions at the borderline between two sciences (but bearing contributions to NLP. The topics of the accepted submissions include:
- Adding Linguistic Knowledge to NLP Tasks
- Multilingual Complex Word Identification
- Text Normalisation
- Text Classification for Social Media
- Automatic Speech Recognition
- Named Entity Recognition
- Part-Of-Speech Tagging
- Cross-Lingual Coreference
- Content-Based Recommender Systems for Books
- Corpora and Processing Tools
- Question Answering, Machine Reading Comprehension

Our authors have a rich variety of nationalities and affiliation countries: Bulgaria, USA, Russia, India, Kazakhstan, Germany, Ireland, Switzerland, Saudi Arabia and Spain.

We are thankful to the members of the Programme Committee for having provided such exhaustive reviews and even accepting additional reviews, and to the conference mentors, who provided additional comments to participants.

Venelin Kovatchev, Irina Temnikova, Branislava Šandrih, and Ivelina Nikolova

Organisers of the Student Research Workshop, special track of the International Conference RANLP 2019

Organizers:

Venelin Kovatchev (Universitat de Barcelona)
Irina Temnikova (freelancer)
Branislava Šandrih (Belgrade University)
Ivelina Nikolova (Bulgarian Academy of Sciences, Bulgaria, Ontotext AD)

Programme Committee:

Aleksandar Savkov (Babylon Health)
Corina Forascu (University "Al. I. Cuza" Iaşi)
Darina Gold (University of Duisburg-Essen)
Diego Moussallem (Paderborn University)
Dmitry Ilvovsky (Higher School of Economics)
Eduardo Blanco (University of North Texas)
Horacio Rodriguez (Universitat Politècnica de Catalunya)
Josef Steinberger (University of West Bohemia)
Liviu P. Dinu (University of Bucharest)
M. Antonia Marti (Universitat de Barcelona)
Mariona Taulé (Universitat de Barcelona)
Navid Rekabsaz (Idiap Research Institute)
Paolo Rosso (Universitat Politècnica de Valencia)
Sandra Kübler (Indiana University Bloomington)
Shervin Malmasi (Harvard Medical School)
Sobha Lalitha Devi (AU-KBC Research Centre)
Thierry Declerck (DFKI GmbH)
Tracy Holloway King (A9.com, Stanford University)
Vijay Sundar Ram (AU-KBC Research Centre, MIT Campus of Anna University)
Yannis Korkontzelos (Edge Hill University)

Table of Contents

Normalization of Kazakh Texts

Assina Abdussaitova
Suleyman Demirel University
Computer Science
Kazakhstan, Kaskelen
assina.abdussaitova@gmail.com

Alina Amangeldiyeva
Suleyman Demirel University
Computer Science
Kazakhstan, Kaskelen
ali099838@gmail.com

Abstract

Kazakh, like other agglutinative languages, has specific difficulties on both recognition of wrong words and generation the corrections for misspelt words. The main goal of this work is to develop a better algorithm for the normalization of Kazakh texts based on traditional and machine learning methods, as well as the new approach which is also considered in this paper. The procedure of election among methods of normalization has been conducted in a manner of comparative analysis. The results of the comparative analysis turned up successful and are shown in detail.

1 Introduction

The Kazakh is a Turkic language which belongs to the Kipchak branch of the Ural-Altaic language family. It is an agglutinative language and differs from other languages like English in the way lexical forms are generated. Since the roots of Kazakh words may make thousands (or even millions) of valid forms which never appear in the dictionary, it has a complex structure such as inflectional and derivational morphology. The topic of analysis of Kazakh was not considered deeply enough; therefore, only a few works were accomplished in building tools in this field. Being one of the oldest problems in Natural Language Processing (NLP) with arguably the highest demand for a practical solution, automatic normalization is one of the necessary steps in text-processing for any language. This paper presents an approach for normalization in agglutinative languages that is based on a combination of error-detection, error-classification and ill-formed word correction methods that take advantage of statistical and rule-based approaches. Note that these developments also consider emoticons (emoji), stylistic uniquenesses (hashtag mention), mixed case problems and more. The main goal is to select the suitable normalization algorithm for Kazakh

texts by comparison-analysis of Levenshtein and Naive-Bayesian algorithms for the case of spelling correction. Since the morphology of the Kazakh consists of unique features, the creation of a reliable model for text transformation, including standard dialects, slangs and emotional spelling errors, will also be a part of the problem. Today, there is no such data sources that can provide with non-dictionary words, except national historical texts and belles-lettres, that is why the new survey has been conducted. The poll has been held among 18-55 aged interviewers. As the survey itself, it has been divided into three parts:

- General questions about most frequently used Kazakh words

- Questions about local-area dialects and slangs

- Questions about wrongly carved words and shortenings

During this survey, the most commonly used words, including ill-formed and spoken words, were gathered. Moreover, the dataset has been collected by parsing websites with the massive amount of Kazakh texts such that commentaries, blog posts, quotes, articles and stories. Therefore, the dataset is provided not only by Kazakh national historical texts and poems, but also parsed comments from Kazakh websites, news blogs, and data gathered by questionnaire. In general, the approximate size of the dataset was about 110 thousand words, including 6% of the survey results, 72% of the parsed data and 22% of the dictionary words from literature and historical texts.

After performing a preliminary study of the normalization tools and Kazakh grammar with morphology, some problems of a misspelling for agglutinative languages in general and Kazakh, in particular, have been pointed out. Through the whole paper, the information about normalization

1

Proceedings of the Student Research Workshop associated with RANLP-2019, pages 1–6,
Varna, Bulgaria, Sep 2–4, 2019.
https://doi.org/10.26615/issn.2603-2821.2019_001

technique, used approaches, obtained results have been considered, and analyses were conducted. For languages with a reasonably straightforward morphology recognition may be reduced to a trivial dictionary lookup: If a given the word is absent from the dictionary, then most likely it has an error. The classification algorithm is divided into two tasks: Error-type recognition and error correction. This process is done through passing the list of selected mistakes: Mixed/upper cases, hashtag mention, emoji, vowel repetition, consonant repetition, vowels absence and non-Cyrillic letters usage.

The contribution can be summarized in two ways: (i) the normalization system has been created for Kazakh texts by improving already existed spelling correction algorithms (ii) based on the methodology used, a website with normalization tool was developed.

The paper is organized as follows. Section 2 reviews related work; after that, the normalization system's algorithm for Kazakh is fully covered in Section 3. Analysis and evaluation are discussed in Section 4. Finally, conclusion and future works are described in Sections 5 and 6.

2   Related Work

There are many works performed on the general spelling correction problem. A lot of approaches were based on comparing a misspelt word with words in a lexicon and suggesting as possible corrections the ones with the minimal edit distance (Damerau, 1964; Levenshtein, 1966). Makazhanov and Makhambetov (Makazhanov et al., 2014) have researched spelling-correction by using the Levenshtein algorithm. According to them, there are two tasks for spelling-correction: Word recognition and error recognition. Hal and Baldwin (Han and Baldwin, 2011) also divided text normalization into two tasks: Ill-formed word detection and candidate word generation. A classical approach to spelling correction for agglutinative languages is to use FSAs (Alegria et al., 2008; Oflazer and Guzey, 1994; Pirinen et al., 2012). Oflazer and Guzey have presented a spelling correction algorithm for agglutinative languages by using finite state automata(FSA). In the proposed method, candidate words are generated using two-level transducers. To optimize the recognizer, the authors prune the paths that generate the substrings of the candidate words which do not pass

some editing distance threshold. In a more recent work presented by Pirinen (Pirinen et al., 2012), the authors use two weighted FSAs one for language model and second for error model, where the authors reorder corrections by using POS n-gram probabilities for a given the word. Recently, another approach is often used (Church and Gale, 1991; Wood, 2013) that is based on applying a noisy channel model (Damerau, 1964), which consists of a source model and a channel model. These works differ in the way how authors weigh the edit operations and in context-awareness of the source models. Researchers Church and Gale (Church and Gale, 1991) utilize word trigram model, while Mays (Pirinen et al., 2012) do not consider the context. Later Brill and Moore (Brill and Moore, 2000) proposed an improved technique with more subtle error model, where instead of using single insertions, deletions, substitutions and transpositions, the authors model substitutions of up to 5- letter sequences that also depend on the position in the word. Hodge and Austin (Hodge and Austin, 2002) proposed an interesting method based on neural system AURA. They have employed two correlation matrix memories: one trained on patterns derived from handling typing errors by binary Hamming distance and n-grams shifting, and another trained on patterns derived from handling phonetic spelling errors. The list of suggested corrections is accomplished by choosing the maximum score obtained from the addition of the scores for Hamming distance and n-grams shifting with the score for phonetic modules. In 2018 Slamova and Mukhanova proposed the keyboard model of spelling correction for Kazakh which was based on replacement rules as a regular expression pattern (Slamova and Mukhanova, 2018).

This paper differs in the way it does spelling corrections. The method for this was combined by mentioned above approaches: Levenshtein and Naive-Bayes. However, these algorithms were used not only by already suggested methods (word recognition, error recognition, ill-formed word detection, candidate word generation, FSTs) but also newly added classification algorithm's techniques to each approach that are further described in the section 3. Normalization algorithm itself is described by more error-types corrections. All in all, this paper focuses on three broad algorithms: Extended classical normalization, normalization based on the Levenshtein and Naive-Bayes algorithms. Each of them will be described in detail further and obtained during the paper results, which, obviously, are more accurate and stronger than in past methods, would be also described and compared.

3 Normalization Algorithms Methodology

Primarily the term normalization means not only spelling correction but also emotional letter repetition, specific characters or symbols use (such that '@', ''), emojis and so on. The full list of error-types is shown below (word in Kazakh, English transcription, English translation):

- Mixed-case/Upper-case ('АспАН', ['aspan'], 'sky')

- Emoticons (':-)')

- Vowel repetition ('аааaспаан', ['aspan'], 'sky')

- Consonant repetition ('солллай', ['solay'], 'so')

- Absence of vowels ('жқс', ['zhaqsy'], 'good')

- Non-verbal symbols and characters ('@example')

During the research, three main approaches have been used: Normalization based on the Levenshtein, Levenshtein with classification rules and Naive-Bayes algorithms. The main task was to compare three algorithms and select the better one, which is more appropriate for the particularities of the Kazakh language. The texts have been tokenized into words by using finite state transducer (Kessikbayeva and Cicekli, 2014) Implementation of FST has been applied by Foma programming language. Since the phrase generation for the Kazakh language differs from other languages, the syllabification based on FST was also used, which divides a word into the root and adjacent endings (Figure 1).

3.1 Normalization Based on the Levenshtein Algorithm

Since the Levenshtein algorithm is mainly presented as the spelling corrector, based on the minimal distance calculation, some problems like

Kazakh	English
дос	friend
достар	friends
досым	my friend
достарым	my friends
достарымнан	from my friends

Figure 1: Features of word formation in the Kazakh in comparison with English

vowel repetition are usually wrongly corrected. Therefore it was decided to add three more steps before implementing it to improve the original model:

1. Classification

2. Preliminary correction of the error

3. Pretest of spelling

The first step is to recognize whether the word has an error or not and, if it does, to classify the type of error (one of six common types of failures listed in Section 3). It should be noted, that usually, there can be more than one error in a word, for example, the word "OooOH" which means "ten" and has two types of errors:

- Mixed case problem

- Emotional vowel repetitive

Therefore, this step returns the list of types of detected errors. After the classification step, the preliminary error-correction is triggered. This step replaces the corrected word according to the list of detected errors. The third step involves an initial check of the spelling of the word before passing the Levenshtein algorithm. If after the third step, the word is still ill-formed, the fourth step is triggered, which is the Levenshtein algorithm. Levenshtein algorithm is based on the distance between two strings source and target (Wood, 2013). The main idea is to measure the difference between two sequences. Mathematical interpretation of the Levenshtein distance is implemented as a matrix, where $M(i,j)$ is the function that calculates the minimum value between the executed operations (Damerau, 1964).

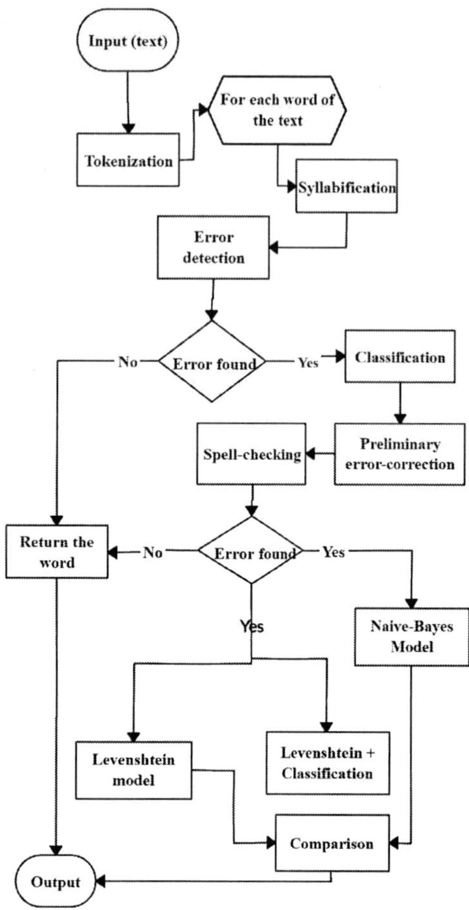

Figure 2: System architecture of the text normalization for Kazakh

When the distances for all targets are calculated, the next step is to choose the appropriate one. Formally, the shortest distance is selected as the best option.

3.2 Normalization Based on the Naive-Bayes Algorithm

The next algorithm is the Naive-Bayes, which is based on classifiers applying Bayes theorem with strong (naive) independence assumptions between the features. Bayes theorem describes the probability of an event based on prior knowledge of conditions that might be related to the event. Mathematically, the Bayes theorem is presented by the following expression:

$$P(A \mid B) = \frac{P(B \mid A)\, P(A)}{P(B)}$$

Here $P(A|B)$ - is a conditional probability showing how often an event A occurs given that B occurs. $P(B|A)$ - is a conditional probability showing how often an event B occurs given that A happens, this is an error model which denotes a likelihood of B being transformed into A. $P(A)$ - is a source model that indicates how likely A is on its own. $P(B)$ - is characteristic for all suggestions denominator that shows how possible B is on its own.

The goal of this paper is to find the probability of correctness of a given word. Since there is a list of candidate corrections, it could also be used. Suppose that the correction of A given the original word B is to be found:

$$P(A \mid B)$$

The correction of A should be found which has the greatest value of $P(A|B)$. By substituting Bayes theorem, this is equivalent to:

$$max_a \frac{P(B \mid A)\, P(A)}{P(B)}$$

The correction of A should be found, which has the greatest value of $P(A|B)$. By substituting Bayes theorem, this is equivalent to:

$$max_a \frac{P(B \mid A)\, P(A)}{P(B)}$$

Since $P(B)$ is the same for all kinds of correction, $P(B)$ can be eliminated, the simplified equation looks like:

$$max_a P(B \mid A) P(A)$$

The $P(A)$ is a probability that the proposed correction stands on its own. In this experiment, P(c) will be determined by word ranks in the dictionary. For example, the word "көк" (kok, blue) has a greater probability than "көктем"(koktem, spring) based on words' usage statistics.

$P(B|A)$ is a probability that B would be typed when the user meant A. Said, this is the probability of how likely the user would type B by mistake when A was intended.

The word with maximum probability from all possible words in the dictionary has been chosen. Of course, the word that is having edit distance greater than 1 has a probability of 0. In 3.1 and 3.2, only $P(A)$ was used to checking.

There are many factors of $P(B|A)$ that needs to be taken into account, but since some factors are

Model	Leven-shtein	Leven-shtein + rules	Naive-Bayes
Avg of properly corrected words	5,1	5,9	0,35
Avg of wrongly corrected words	6,15	4,75	0,2
Avg of unnecessary corrected words	6,1	1,4	0,05
Precision	93,58	96,85	99,19
Recall	46,36	56,42	81,33
f1 score	*62*	*71,3*	*89,38*

Table 1: Testing results of 3 models for normalization

not entirely independent (increasing probability of x may decrease the probability of y), the simple analysis through it was made.

4 Analysis

Since three approaches have been selected, there are three stages of testing: Levenshtein-based algorithm, Levenshtein plus classification rules based algorithm and Naive-Bayes based algorithm. Twenty different experiments for each model with a variety of cases have been conducted. Each test consisted of sentences with 20-25 words, 11 of which were ill-formed at the average, at which point the average precision and recall have been calculated. The average records for each testing section are shown in figure 3, where the f1 score is the accuracy of the considered models. The first block of the table describes the results of Levenshtein spelling-correction algorithm-based model. F1 score for this model turned out only 62% with 46,36% of recall value. The next model (Levenshtein + classification rules algorithm) showed up quite higher than the first - 71,3% of the f1 score and 56,42% of recall gives almost 10% breakaway from original Levenshtein algorithm.

Finally, the third model, which is based on Machine Learning Naive-Bayes algorithm gave the highest results compared with others. Its f1 score reached 89,38% which is 27,38% more than the original and 18,08% models. According to the precision values, Naive-Bayesian model is also the leader - 99,19%. One of the reasons for that lies on the large dataset, which was gathered by parsing websites and conducting the surveys. To compare, testing results of the model proposed by Slamova and Mukhanova has accuracy 85.4% (Slamova and Mukhanova, 2018).

5 Conclusion

In this paper, the normalization tool for Kazakh texts based on a Machine Learning algorithm has been developed. According to the results, this tool outperforms other analogs with spelling corrector based on Levenshtein-distance. Finally, the high overall accuracy in generating correct suggestions was received. The difference between normalization and spelling corrector lies in new added conditions and cases that expand the possibilities of normalization and increase the probability of words correctness. For instance, no research and tool consider the list of mistakes in the Kazakh language, which was suggested in this paper. The advantage of the proposed new method is that it can be iteratively improved by adding new rules/transitions to the normalization and new entries to the root lexicon. Moreover, the Bayesian approach, which is the core of this method, can also be used for morphological segmentation.

6 Future Works

Some areas need to be considered deeper in the future. In particular, this is the complete data for Kazakh dictionary taken from common knowledge of people (related to mother language and geographical area), list of frequently occurring slang, specific words are still in progress and should be enlarged, since for Kazakh language there are no big data sources of training data as opposed to resources in English. Moreover, after the process of gathering data, it will be necessary to analyze and structure it. Also, many aspects are needed to be taken into account to improve the effectiveness of normalization, such as:

1. Number of common and obscure words in the dictionary

2. Type of keyboard and its distance between two specific characters

3. Edit-distance (greater than 1 or 0, even though edit-distance of 1 has covered at least 80 per cent of correctness probability)

4. Word structures (the Kazakh language has a big number of endings with different roots)

Another further research question will be about the combination of Levenshtein and Naive-Bayesian algorithms. The future work will be directed towards answering this question, as well as incorporating context sensitivity into the method used and improvements that could be applied based on this research work.

Acknowledgments

Special gratitude is expressed to those who contributed to this work through suggestions, criticism and review. Special thanks to anonymous reviewers, as well as Gulshat Kessikbayeva, a professor at Suleyman Demirel University, and Nazerke Sultanova, a teacher.

References

I. Alegria, K. Ceberio, N. Ezeiza, A. Soroa, and G. Hernandez. 2008. Spelling correction : from two- level morphology to open source. in: Lrec, european language resources association. 4:1051–1054.

E. Brill and R. Moore. 2000. Proceedings of the 38th annual meeting of the association for computational linguistics. Association for Computational Linguistics.

K. Church and W. Gale. 1991. *Probability scoring for spelling correction. Statistics and Computing.*

F. Damerau. 1964. A technique for computer detection and correction of spelling errors. pages 171–176.

B. Han and T. Baldwin. 2011. Lexical normalisation of short text messages. pages 368–378.

V. Hodge and J. Austin. 2002. A comparison of a novel neural spell checker and standard spell checking algorithms. pages 2571–2580.

Gulshat Kessikbayeva and Ilyas Cicekli. 2014. Rule based morphological analyzer of kazakh language. *Proceedings of the 2014 Joint Meeting of SIGMORPHON and SIGFSM.*

V. Levenshtein. 1966. Binary codes capable of correcting deletions, insertions and reversals. 2:707–710.

A. Makazhanov, O. Makhambetov, I. Sabyrgaliyev, and Z. Yessenbayev. 2014. Spelling correction for kazakh. computational linguistics and intelligent text processing. pages 533–541.

K. Oflazer and C. Guzey. 1994. Spelling correction in agglutinative languages. 2:194–195.

T. Pirinen, M. Silfverberg, and K. Linden. 2012. Improving finite-state spell-checker suggestions with part of speech n-grams.

Gaukhar Slamova and Meruyert Mukhanova. 2018. Text normalization and spelling correction in kazakh language. In *AIST*.

Z. Wood. 2013. Profiling spatial collectives. research and development in intelligent systems. 2:102–103.

Classification Approaches to Identify Informative Tweets

Piush Aggarwal
University of Duisburg-Essen
`piush.aggarwal@stud.uni-due.de`

Abstract

Social media platforms have become prime forums for reporting news with users sharing what they saw, heard or read on social media. News from social media is potentially useful for various stakeholders including aid organizations, news agencies, and individuals. However, social media also contains a vast amount of non-news content. For users to be able to draw on benefits from news reported on social media it is necessary to reliably identify news content and differentiate it from non-news. In this paper, we tackle the challenge of classifying a social post as news or not. To this end, we provide a new manually annotated dataset containing 2,992 tweets from 5 different topical categories. Unlike earlier datasets, it includes postings posted by personal users who do not promote a business or a product and are not affiliated with any organization. We also investigate various baseline systems and evaluate their performance on the newly generated dataset. Our results show that the best classifiers are the SVM and BERT models.

1 Introduction

In the last decade, social media have become the platform par excellence for all kinds of online information exchange, such as content creation, consumption, and sharing; commenting on and engaging with contents posted by others. During unwanted situations like natural calamities, accidents, etc., users provide informative postings on social media websites to report about the incidents, to share an update about them and inform others about what they saw, heard or read.

In this case, the users play the role of journalists and report the news to the public. However, there is also a vast amount of data that does not contain news-like information such as personal information, chats among friends, etc. Analyzing social media posts for whether they are news or not would allow e.g. aid providers during natural calamities to determine relevant information and plan appropriate actions. Furthermore, journalists could use such analysis to determine newsworthy information or even gain updates about events they have been reporting.

This paper contributes to the task of classifying social media posts, specifically Twitter messages, as news or non-news by providing data and a set of benchmark results for the task. The main contribution of the paper includes dataset[1] containing 2992 tweets manually labeled as *news* or *not*. To the best of our knowledge, related datasets are either event specific (Freitas and Ji, 2016) or queried with news-related keywords or hashtags like the name of news agencies (Liu et al., 2017). Unlike these datasets, our data consists of news reported by individual users and not just specific to tweets posted by news agencies. The dataset is developed to include tweets coming from first-hand reporters and witnesses of an event, which would be useful in the aforementioned scenarios. Although these first-hand reports can be very important in a given situation, the tweets coming from individuals are not identified as news by hashtags and are therefore more difficult to classify as news or not, in particular as individual tweets are more likely than organizational ones to report personal information. Furthermore, our dataset contains a variety of topics, unlike previously reported data which is focused on an event. We also investigate the behaviour of the dataset, find patterns and regulari-

---

[1] `https://github.com/aggarwalpiush/`
`goodBadNewsTweet`

Proceedings of the Student Research Workshop associated with RANLP-2019, pages 7–15,
Varna, Bulgaria, Sep 2–4, 2019.
https://doi.org/10.26615/issn.2603-2821.2019_002

ties using text visualisations.

For news classification, we adopt a supervised machine learning paradigm and report the performance of seven classifiers, which can be used as baselines in future work. We report the results of SVM (Chang and Lin, 2011), Logistic Regression (Fan et al., 2008), Random Forest (Breiman, 2001), Decision Tree (Breiman et al., 1984) and Xgboost classifier (Chen and Guestrin, 2016). In addition to shallow learning approaches, we train a Multi-Layer-Perceptron (MLP) model (Hinton, 1989) and also we use the pre-trained BERT-base model (Devlin et al., 2018). In the end, we claim the usabilty of our dataset by performing cross-domain experiments.

In this paper, we first discuss the related work (Section 2). In Section 3 we describe the dataset which we plan to make publicly available. In Section 4, we describe our experiments and present the results of the baseline systems used. We conclude and outline our future directions in Section 5.

2   Related Work

A widely accepted analysis of news values are defined by Galtung and Ruge's twelve news factors (Harcup and ONeill, 2017). According to this research, generally, a news story should be selected if it is published in context of potential figures, celebrity or organisation, fulfilling public need and interest, related to curiosity and amazement, a propaganda, positive-negative events, focusing on a huge crowd or relevant to the audience. In the last few years, there have been several studies published on the application of computational methods in order to identify news from tweets. Sankaranarayanan et al. (2009) built a news processing system, called *TwitterStand* using an unsupervised approach to classify tweets collected from pre-determined users who frequently post news about events. Sriram et al. (2010) use lexical and structural features based multi-class classification on manually annotated tweets having different categories (including *news*). Castillo et al. (2011) investigate tweet newsworthiness classification using features representing the message, user, topic and the propagation of messages. Others use features based on social influence, information propagation, syntactic and combinations of local linguistic features as well as user history and user opinion to select informative tweets (Inouye and

Kalita, 2011; Yang et al., 2011; Li et al., 2012; Ren et al., 2013; Chua and Asur, 2013). Freitas and Ji (2016) use content based features like slang usage, sentiment terms, etc. to identify newsworthy tweets. Liu et al. (2017) use unsupervised approaches like clustering to identify news related topics among twitter postings. We differ from related work in various aspects. First, our dataset consists of tweets not specific to news agencies. Messages posted by news agencies can be easily tracked using e.g. the news agencies' hashtags. However, news posts reported by normal users will not have such hashtags and are difficult to determine. Next, such normal user-generated contents are of more value since they are the first source of information and tracking and knowing about them can e.g. in natural disaster situations be life-saving. Furthermore, our dataset is not specific to a particular topic but contains tweets from 5 different categories that are topically not related. Finally, we investigate various supervised techniques on this dataset to provide the community with various baselines.

Label	Tweet
News	*Indian cities and towns became less clean after Prime Minister Narendra Modi's Swaach Bharat mission*
News	*Unsafe abortion could induce some health related implications such as health risks to the girl or woman including #HUV/AIDS risks and #STDs*
Not News	*@chamberlainusoh If #Ebola has no known cure, what's then the need of going to the hospital*
Not News	*Honestly: ambient intelligence is a concept in the Internet of Things. But really do we want soo much controll handed over to devices?*

Table 1: Examples of news and not-news tweets

3   Dataset

Our dataset contains tweets labelled as news or not. Tweets are collected from five different categories and get the labels using crowd-source experiments. For annotation instructions, we sum-

Category	Topics	Collected	Annotated
Health	Ebola	90,430	287
	HIV	31,566	275
Natural Disaster	Hurricane Harvey	1,458,000	304
	Hurricane Irma	4,698,000	302
Terrorist Attack	Macerata oohmm	492,159	297
	Stockholm Attack	344,396	307
Geography and Env.	AGU17	29,997	310
	Swachh Bharat	19,868	283
Science and Edu.	IOT	6,326,806	319
	Nintendo	104,695	308

Table 2: Categories, their topics and distributions for the dataset generation

marised Galtung and Ruge's (Harcup and ONeill, 2017) twelve news factors and consider a text statement as news story if it holds informative elements or noticeable events. Similarly, tweets with no informative content are considered as not newsworthy. Table 1 illustrate examples of *news* and *not news*. With this, we believe to have a simple and sophisticated annotation task.

Data Collection   Our data contain tweets from 5 categories with which we aim to have wider topic coverage. Furthermore, for each category, two different sub-topics are chosen to make the dataset more diverse. The first and second columns of Table 2 represent categories and their corresponding topics.

To collect the data, we used the following strategies. For the health category, for *Ebola* tweets, we used tweet-ids provided by Tamine et al. (2016) and for *HIV*, we used different hashtags shown in Table 3. For the natural disaster category, we collected *Hurricane Harvey* and *Irma* tweets from Littman (2017). From Tweet Catalog portal[2], we collected tweets related to *Macerata* and *Stockholm attack*. We use *AGU17* tweets from Pikas (2018) and for *Swachh Bharat Abhiyan* (Clean India Campaign), we looked for tweets containing hashtags shown in the second row of Table 3. For *IOT*, we used tweets from Bian et al. (2016) and for *Nintendo*, we used one of the kaggle datasets[3] which consists of tweets that were collected during the Nintendo E3 2018 Conference. The third column of Table 2 represents number of tweets collected for the aforementioned topics.

Topic	Hash-Tags
Hiv	#AIDS, #aids, #hiv, #HIV, #PLHIV, #StopHIV, #EndAIDS, #HIVTreatmentWorks
SB	#MyCleanIndia, #SwachhBharat, #SwachhBharatSwasthBharat, #Killpollution, #SwachhBharatSwasthBharat

Table 3: Hashtags for tweets collection (here SB refers to *Swachh Bharat*)

Data Annotation   From the collected tweets, we first filtered out all the tweets which are not in English language. Then we removed re-tweets and finally removed duplicates based on lower-cased first four words of tweets keeping only the first one, then we randomly pick 500 tweets from each topic.

To annotate tweets whether they are *news* or *not* we used the crowd-sourcing platform Figure Eight[4]. We showed each annotator 5 tweets per page and paid 3 US Cents per tweet. To ensure quality, we used 125 test questions created by 5 different annotators[5]. In addition to the test questions, we applied a restriction so that annotation could be performed only by people from English speaking countries. We also made sure that each annotation was performed maximum by 7 annotators and that an annotator agreement of min. 70%

---

[2] https://www.docnow.io/catalog/
[3] http://tiny.cc/iookbz

[4] https://figure-eight.com

[5] These are non-crowd annotators. All are post-graduate students and use Twitter to post information on a daily basis. We considered a tweet as test instance if at least 4 annotators agreed on the class label.

was met. Note if the agreement of 70% was met with fewer annotators then the system would not force an annotation to be done by 7 annotators but would finish earlier. The system requires 7 annotators if the minimum agreement requirement is not met. We only choose instances which are annotated by at least 3 annotators. In addition to the news and not news categories, we also allowed a third category, namely *not sure*. We filtered out tweets where annotators were unsure about their judgment. We use a total 5000 tweets to annotate. Of these, 2992 were classified as news or not news. The other 2008 tweets were discarded because the annotators were not sure about their decision. The topic-wise number of successful annotations are displayed in the fourth column of Table 2. Further, we randomly split the resulting dataset into train and test set. Table 4 shows the distribution of each set.

Label	Train	Test	Total
NEWS	756	253	1,009
NOT NEWS	1,731	252	1,983
All	2487	505	2,992

Table 4: Dataset distribution

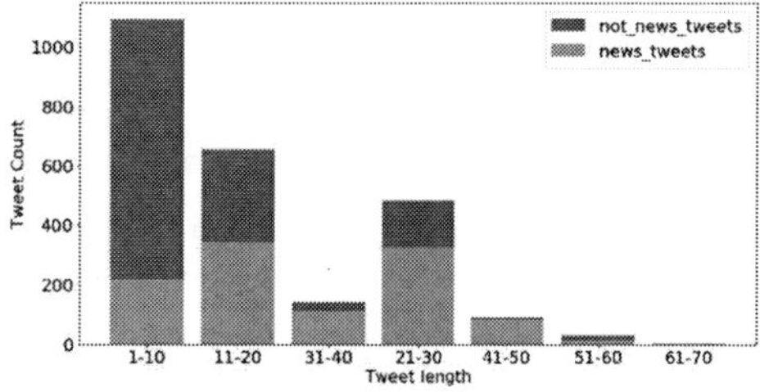

Figure 1: Length based distribution of tweets labelled with news and not news

Inter Annotator Agreement To evaluate the quality of the annotation, we compute Fleiss' kappa (Fleiss, 1971) scores between the annotators. For test questions, we record a kappa of 0.522, which indicates good agreement. For instances uploaded to the crowdsource platform, the majority class label for each tweet is collected and we compared it to the labels provided by the annotators. Such strategy is also followed by earlier studies (Zubiaga et al., 2016). In the end, an agreement of 0.443 is recorded, indicating a moderate

Not News	News
new orleans	*tropical storm*
stay safe	*african migrants*
hope everyone	*italy attack*
blog post	*northern league*
please stay	*target immigrants*
safe everyone	*attack targets*
go time	*tropical depression*
new blog	*caribbean sea*

Table 5: List of most frequent bi-grams in the *news* and *not-news* corpora

agreement among the annotators.

Data Analysis To analyse the generated dataset, we perform several experiments (Mien, 2017) that visualise differences in the behaviour of news and not-news tweets. Also, the analysis helps in finding patterns and regularity among the data which certainly play a major role for deciding features and the further classification process. Before experimentation, we pre-processed the generated dataset by removing numbers, stop-words and tweet specific keywords like *hiv*, *macerata*, etc. from the tweet texts and lower-cased them. First, we analyse tweet length distribution for each tweet label. In Figure 1, each bar presents the tweet count for each label with respect to the word length interval. From the Figure, it can be concluded that *news* tweets are much less frequent than *not news* tweets if their length is less than 10 words, but as the length of the tweets get increases, *news* tweets become dominant over *not news* ones.

To learn about the number and kind of topics present in a body of text, two tweet corpora are created by concatenating the tweet posts for each label (*news* and *not news*) and most frequent bi-grams are extracted (see Table 5). From the Table, we can see, *not news* tweets generally focus on conversation related words whereas newsworthy tweets include instances associated with events, group references, etc.

We also find some of the terms which are frequently available in both text corpora. We plot lexical dispersion which displays occurrence of terms with respect to word offset in the corpus[6]. Each word on the y-axis has a strip representing the entire text in terms of offset, and a mark on the strip indicates the occurrence of the word at that off-

---

[6]taking only the first 10,000 terms for each corpus

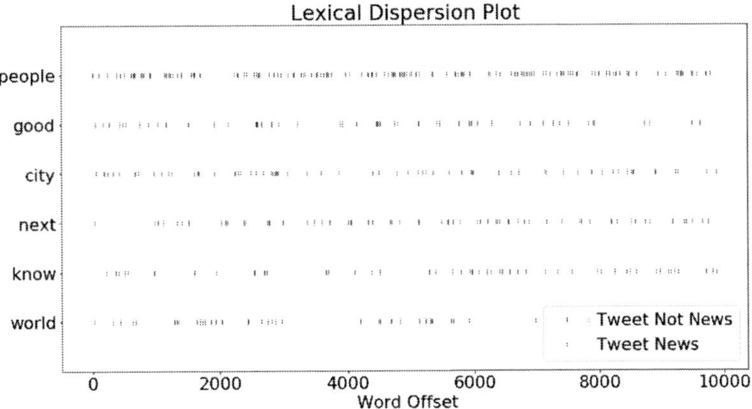

Figure 2: Lexical dispersion distribution of commonly used terms found in the Twitter corpus annotated with news and not news labels

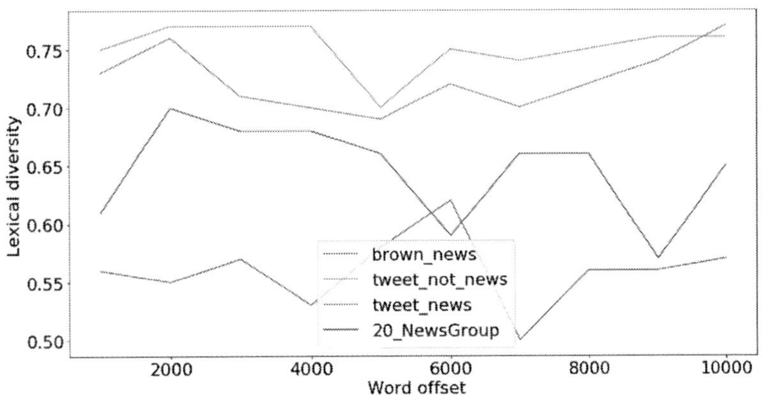

Figure 3: Lexical diversity distribution of different corpora dispersed on word offset interval

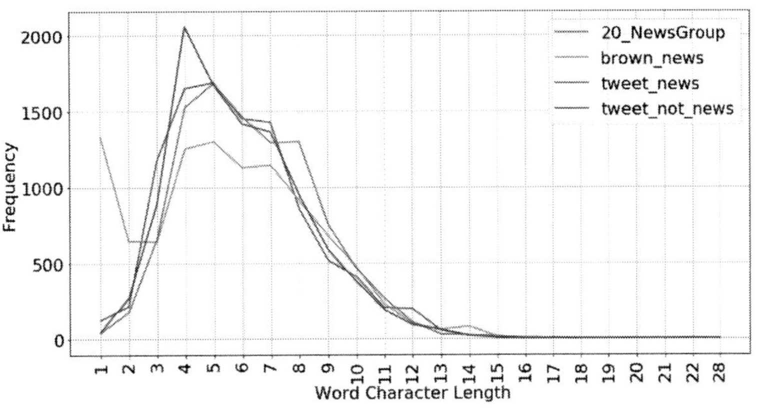

Figure 4: Word's character length distribution for different corpora

set. Analysis shows that there are very few news tweets which contain *good* and *know* terms. However, terms like *people* and *city* are equally dispersed among the tweets in both categories (news and not news).

Lexical diversity (ld) distribution of the generated dataset is also analysed, which can be defined for the given text t as:

$$ld = \frac{count\ of\ unique\ words\ in\ t}{count\ of\ total\ words\ in\ t} \qquad (1)$$

For analysing the lexical diversity (Johansson, 2008), first 10,000 terms for each tweet corpus are taken and divide them into chunks of size 1000 words. For each chunk, ld is calculated (Equation 1) and plotted it with respect to word offset intervals as shown in Figure 3.

We also plot the same distribution for two well-known news corpora. The first corpus (also called 20-NewsGroup[7]) comprises around 18000 newsgroups posts on 20 topics. For the other corpus (Brown Corpus[8]), we focus only on news genre which include news from 44 different categories. From Figure 3, it can be interpreted that lexical diversity for news-related corpora (brown_news, tweet_news and 20_NewsGroup) is low compared to not news tweet corpora.

We also analyse the distribution of word length in terms of the number of characters and compare it among different corpora as discussed above. We took a subset of each corpus (first 10,000 terms) and plot the frequency of each word length for each corpus (see Figure 4). The figure illustrate that in not news tweets, most words have a length of (size) 4 whereas in news corpora most words hold 5 characters.

Finally, we tried to figure out the n-gram distribution pattern among different corpora. We plot n-gram distribution for each corpus (see Figure 5) where n is 1 to 5. In the Figure, the x-axis has different values of n-grams and the y-axis has the number of times the n-gram has occurred[9]. The figure shows that news instances of tweets capture more bi-grams than not-news ones.

---

[7]http://qwone.com/~jason/20Newsgroups/
[8]http://tiny.cc/bytkbz
[9]here only those n-grams are chosen which are occurred more than 1 time.

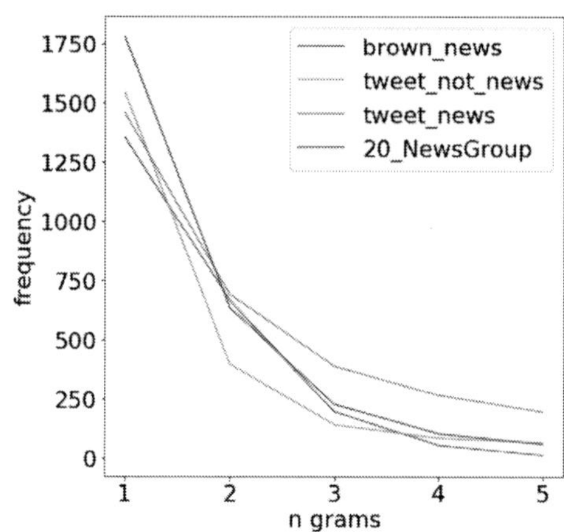

Figure 5: N-gram frequency distribution for corpora

4 Experiments and Results

As our task is to identify whether a particular tweet is news or not, we treat it as a binary classification task. We train our baseline classifiers on the training set and evaluate the resulting models on the test set where label distribution is in proportion with that of training set (see Table 4 for the training and testing split).

Preprocessing and Feature Extraction   Tweets are lower-cased and use Ark Tokenizer (Gimpel et al., 2011) for segmentation. After these preprocessing steps, we represent each posting by a dense embedding, created by the mean of the individual words embeddings. We use the pre-trained embeddings provided by (Mikolov et al., 2018), which are trained on the common crawl corpus. In addition to posting embeddings, we also extract syntactic features in the form of TF-IDF vectors (Salton and McGill, 1986) for up to 3 grams having vocabulary size as vector dimensions.

Baseline Classifiers   To classify *news* and *not news* we train the following classifiers: SVM (Chang and Lin, 2011) with regularization parameter (C) as 10 and rbf as kernel, Logistic Regression (Fan et al., 2008) with 0.1 as inverse regularization strength, Random Forest (Breiman, 2001) with 15 as maximum depth and 500 trees. We use Decision Tree (Breiman et al., 1984) with 2 minimum sample leaves and 3 as minimum sample split and Xgboost classifier (Chen and Guestrin,

Approach	Embeddings			TF-IDF(1-3 gram)		
	Precision	Recall	F_1	Precision	Recall	F_1
SVM	**.854**	**.851**	**.851**	.808	.808	.808
BERT	.835	.841	.838	-	-	-
Random Forest	.839	.838	.837	**.821**	**.820**	**.820**
Logit Reg.	.828	.827	.827	.812	.812	.812
Xgboost	.823	.822	.822	.802	.794	.792
MLP Classifier	.801	.772	.767	.809	.794	.791
Decision Tree	.733	.733	.733	.755	.754	.754
Majority Vote - all NOT	.331	.500	.399	.331	.500	.399

Table 6: Classifiers evaluation results

2016). In addition to shallow learning approaches, we train a model called Multi-Layer-Perceptron (MLP) (Hinton, 1989) with Sigmoid activation function (Cybenko, 1989), 0.001 as l2 penalty (Ng, 2004), adaptive as learning rate (Schaul and LeCun, 2013) and 0.1 as tolerance. Apart from the mentioned hyper-parameters, we use default-parameters provided by scikit-learn (Pedregosa et al., 2011). Finally, we use the pre-trained BERT-base model (Devlin et al., 2018) to create a vector representation of a posting. We fine-tune the model on the training dataset using a sequence length of 64 and batches of 32 and training epochs of 2.

Evaluation and Results We evaluate the performance of the classifiers using the test set (Table 4). We report Precision, Recall, and Macro F_1 (Powers and Ailab, 2011) for all the classifiers. We use the majority class (all-NOT) as the additional baseline. Table 6 shows the performance scores. The results show that the SVM classifier with the posting vector-representation achieves the best F-Score, followed by BERT. Using content based semantic features like word embeddings we were able to achieve better performance than using syntactic based features like TF-IDF vectors.

Dataset Usability Using cross domain experiments, we investigate the practical usability of our dataset where we train our best model on in-domains and test on out-of-domain data. For this purpose, we split the dataset into a training set consisting of all examples that belong to 4 categories and the left out category instances are used to create a held-out test set. We train a SVM classifier with fasttext embeddings on the training set. Figure 6 illustrates the results of the model tested

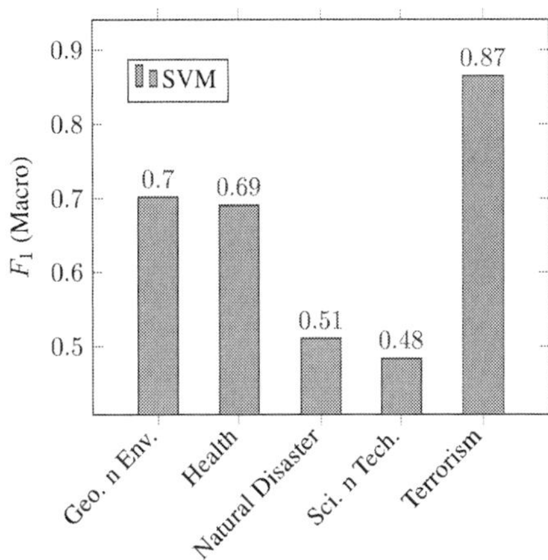

Figure 6: Cross domain performance of SVM for each tweet category

on different domains. The models achieve an average macro F_1 score of 65% which is much higher than the majority class baseline. We also see low F_1 scores in the cases of *Science n Technology* and *Natural Disaster* domains. For Science n Technology, one possible reason is availability of only 2% of true news labels. In case of Natural Disaster, we found 56% news true labels. Therefore, to find the root cause, we perform an experiment where we add a small proportion of out-of-domain data to the training set. We transfer 12% of the instances of Natural Disaster from test-set to train-set. The model achieve an F_1 score of 69% which is a substantial increase from its previous value. The analysis show the practical usability of the dataset. In some cases, model may under-fit, such cases can be handled by adding small amounts of out-of-domain data.

5 Conclusion

In this paper, we release a new dataset containing 2992 tweets annotated as news or not. This dataset will be publicly available for the research community. To the best of our knowledge, this is the first dataset that consists of Twitter postings with 5 diversified categories consisting of postings from first-hand reporters and witnesses of an event, which would be useful in emergency situations such as natural disasters to gain knowledge about the happenings. We experimented with seven different supervised machine learning techniques and showed that best performances can be achieved using the SVM and BERT models. These techniques serve as baselines.

In the future, we would like to put more focus on data augmentation and further categorization of newsworthy tweets as good or bad news.

Acknowledgments

I thank *Dr. Ahmet Aker* (University of Duisburg-Essen) and the anonymous reviewers for their most useful feedback. This work was supported by the Deutsche Forschungsgemeinschaft (DFG) under grant No. ZE 915/7-1 "Data and Knowledge Processing (DKPro) - A middleware for language technology", by the Global Young Faculty[10] and the Deutsche Forschungsgemeinschaft (DFG, German Research Foundation) - GRK 2167, Research Training Group "User-Centred Social Media".

References

Jiang Bian, Kenji Yoshigoe, Amanda Hicks, Jiawei Yuan, Zhe He, Mengjun Xie, Yi Guo, Mattia Prosperi, Ramzi Salloum, and Franois Modave. 2016. Mining Twitter to Assess the Public Perception of the Internet of Things. *PLOS ONE* 11(7):1–14. https://doi.org/10.1371/journal.pone.0158450.

Leo Breiman. 2001. Random Forests. *Machine Learning* 45(1):5–32. https://doi.org/10.1023/A:1010933404324.

Leo Breiman, Jerome H Friedman, Richard A Olshen, and Charles J Stone. 1984. *Classification and regression trees*. The Wadsworth statistics/probability series. Wadsworth and Brooks/Cole Advanced Books and Software, Monterey, CA. http://cds.cern.ch/record/2253780.

Carlos Castillo, Marcelo Mendoza, and Barbara Poblete. 2011. Information Credibility on Twitter. In *Proceedings of the 20th International Conference on World Wide Web*. ACM, New York, NY, USA, WWW '11, pages 675–684. https://doi.org/10.1145/1963405.1963500.

Chih-Chung Chang and Chih-Jen Lin. 2011. LIBSVM: A Library for Support Vector Machines. *ACM Trans. Intell. Syst. Technol.* 2(3):27:1–27:27. https://doi.org/10.1145/1961189.1961199.

Tianqi Chen and Carlos Guestrin. 2016. XGBoost: A Scalable Tree Boosting System. In *Proceedings of the 22nd ACM SIGKDD International Conference on Knowledge Discovery and Data Mining*. ACM, New York, NY, USA, KDD '16, pages 785–794. https://doi.org/10.1145/2939672.2939785.

Freddy Chong Tat Chua and Sitaram Asur. 2013. Automatic summarization of events from social media. In *ICWSM*.

G. Cybenko. 1989. Approximation by superpositions of a sigmoidal function. *Mathematics of Control, Signals and Systems* 2(4):303–314. https://doi.org/10.1007/BF02551274.

Jacob Devlin, Ming-Wei Chang, Kenton Lee, and Kristina Toutanova. 2018. BERT: Pre-training of Deep Bidirectional Transformers for Language Understanding. *arXiv preprint arXiv:1810.04805* .

Rong-En Fan, Kai-Wei Chang, Cho-Jui Hsieh, Xiang-Rui Wang, and Chih-Jen Lin. 2008. LIBLINEAR: A Library for Large Linear Classification. *J. Mach. Learn. Res.* 9:1871–1874. http://dl.acm.org/citation.cfm?id=1390681.1442794.

Joseph L. Fleiss. 1971. Measuring nominal scale agreement among many raters. *Psychological Bulletin* 76(5):378–382. https://doi.org/10.1037/h0031619.

Jesse Freitas and Heng Ji. 2016. Identifying News from Tweets. In *NLP+CSS@EMNLP*.

Kevin Gimpel, Nathan Schneider, Brendan O'Connor, Dipanjan Das, Daniel Mills, Jacob Eisenstein, Michael Heilman, Dani Yogatama, Jeffrey Flanigan, and Noah A. Smith. 2011. Part-of-Speech Tagging for Twitter: Annotation, Features, and Experiments. In *Proceedings of the 49th Annual Meeting of the Association for Computational Linguistics: Human Language Technologies*. Association for Computational Linguistics, pages 42–47. http://aclweb.org/anthology/P11-2008.

Tony Harcup and Deirdre ONeill. 2017. What is News? *Journalism Studies* 18(12):1470–1488. https://doi.org/10.1080/1461670X.2016.1150193.

Geoffrey E. Hinton. 1989. Connectionist learning procedures. *Artificial Intelligence* 40(1):185 – 234. https://doi.org/https://doi.org/10.1016/0004-3702(89)90049-0.

---

[10]https://www.global-young-faculty.de/

David Inouye and Jugal K. Kalita. 2011. Comparing Twitter Summarization Algorithms for Multiple Post Summaries. In *2011 IEEE Third International Conference on Privacy, Security, Risk and Trust and 2011 IEEE Third International Conference on Social Computing*. pages 298–306. https://doi.org/10.1109/PASSAT/SocialCom.2011.31.

V Johansson. 2008. Lexical diversity and lexical density in speech and writing: A developmental perspective. *Lund Working Papers in Linguistics* 53:61–79.

Hao Li, Yu Chen, Heng Ji, Smaranda Muresan, and Dequan Zheng. 2012. Combining Social Cognitive Theories with Linguistic Features for Multigenre Sentiment Analysis. In *Proceedings of the 26th Pacific Asia Conference on Language, Information, and Computation*. Faculty of Computer Science, Universitas Indonesia, pages 127–136. http://aclweb.org/anthology/Y12-1013.

Justin Littman. 2017. Hurricanes Harvey and Irma Tweet ids. https://doi.org/10.7910/DVN/QRKIBW.

Xiaomo Liu, Armineh Nourbakhsh, Quanzhi Li, Sameena Shah, Robert Martin, and John Duprey. 2017. Reuters tracer: Toward automated news production using large scale social media data. In *2017 IEEE International Conference on Big Data (Big Data)*. pages 1483–1493. https://doi.org/10.1109/BigData.2017.8258082.

Mien. 2017. Visual text analytics with python - mien. https://medium.com/@therealmien/visual-text-analytics-with-python-6111ae8b16df.

Tomas Mikolov, Edouard Grave, Piotr Bojanowski, Christian Puhrsch, and Armand Joulin. 2018. Advances in Pre-Training Distributed Word Representations. In *Proceedings of the International Conference on Language Resources and Evaluation (LREC 2018)*.

Andrew Y. Ng. 2004. Feature Selection, L1 vs. L2 Regularization, and Rotational Invariance. In *Proceedings of the Twenty-first International Conference on Machine Learning*. ACM, New York, NY, USA, ICML '04, pages 78–. https://doi.org/10.1145/1015330.1015435.

F. Pedregosa, G. Varoquaux, A. Gramfort, V. Michel, B. Thirion, O. Grisel, M. Blondel, P. Prettenhofer, R. Weiss, V. Dubourg, J. Vanderplas, A. Passos, D. Cournapeau, M. Brucher, M. Perrot, and E. Duchesnay. 2011. Scikit-learn: Machine Learning in Python. *Journal of Machine Learning Research* 12:2825–2830.

Christina Pikas. 2018. American Geophysical Union Annual Meeting Tweets 2017 https://doi.org/10.6084/m9.figshare.5756514.v1.

David M. W. Powers and Ailab. 2011. Evaluation: from Precision, Recall and F-measure to ROC, Informedness, Markedness and Correlation.

Zhaochun Ren, Shangsong Liang, Edgar Meij, and Maarten de Rijke. 2013. Personalized Time-aware Tweets Summarization. In *Proceedings of the 36th International ACM SIGIR Conference on Research and Development in Information Retrieval*. ACM, New York, NY, USA, SIGIR '13, pages 513–522. https://doi.org/10.1145/2484028.2484052.

Gerard Salton and Michael J. McGill. 1986. *Introduction to Modern Information Retrieval*. McGraw-Hill, Inc., New York, NY, USA.

Jagan Sankaranarayanan, Hanan Samet, Benjamin E. Teitler, Michael D. Lieberman, and Jon Sperling. 2009. TwitterStand: News in Tweets. In *Proceedings of the 17th ACM SIGSPATIAL International Conference on Advances in Geographic Information Systems*. ACM, New York, NY, USA, GIS '09, pages 42–51. https://doi.org/10.1145/1653771.1653781.

Tom Schaul and Yann LeCun. 2013. Adaptive learning rates and parallelization for stochastic, sparse, non-smooth gradients. *CoRR* abs/1301.3764. http://arxiv.org/abs/1301.3764.

Bharath Sriram, Dave Fuhry, Engin Demir, Hakan Ferhatosmanoglu, and Murat Demirbas. 2010. Short Text Classification in Twitter to Improve Information Filtering. In *Proceedings of the 33rd International ACM SIGIR Conference on Research and Development in Information Retrieval*. ACM, New York, NY, USA, SIGIR '10, pages 841–842. https://doi.org/10.1145/1835449.1835643.

Lynda Tamine, Laure Soulier, Lamjed Ben Jabeur, Frederic Amblard, Chihab Hanachi, Gilles Hubert, and Camille Roth. 2016. Social Media-Based Collaborative Information Access: Analysis of Online Crisis-Related Twitter Conversations. In *Proceedings of the 27th ACM Conference on Hypertext and Social Media*. ACM, New York, NY, USA, HT '16, pages 159–168. https://doi.org/10.1145/2914586.2914589.

Zi Yang, Keke Cai, Jie Tang, Li Zhang, Zhong Su, and Juanzi Li. 2011. Social Context Summarization. In *Proceedings of the 34th International ACM SIGIR Conference on Research and Development in Information Retrieval*. ACM, New York, NY, USA, SIGIR '11, pages 255–264. https://doi.org/10.1145/2009916.2009954.

Arkaitz Zubiaga, Maria Liakata, Rob Procter, Geraldine Wong Sak Hoi, and Peter Tolmie. 2016. Analysing how people orient to and spread rumours in social media by looking at conversational threads. *PloS one* 11(3):e0150989.

Dialect-Specific Models for Automatic Speech Recognition of African American Vernacular English

Rachel Dorn
Virginia Commonwealth University
`dornrm@mymail.vcu.edu`

Abstract

African American Vernacular English (AAVE) is a widely-spoken dialect of English, yet it is under-represented in major speech corpora. As a result, speakers of this dialect are often misunderstood by NLP applications. This study explores the effect on transcription accuracy of an automatic voice recognition system when AAVE data is used. Models trained on AAVE data and on Standard American English data were compared to a baseline model trained on a combination of the two dialects. The accuracy for both dialect-specific models was significantly higher than the baseline model, with the AAVE model showing over 18% improvement. By isolating the effect of having AAVE speakers in the training data, this study highlights the importance of increasing diversity in the field of natural language processing.

1 Introduction

There have been tremendous improvements in recent years in automatic speech recognition (ASR). Models which approach or even surpass human performance on transcription tasks have been reported (Xiong et al., 2017). However, these increases in accuracy have not been evenly distributed across all speakers, performing worse for speakers of dialects other than Standard American English (SAE) (Tatman and Kasten, 2017). ASR systems are becoming more and more integrated into society, used in everything from call centers to medical transcriptions to asking for the weather. Poorer performance for individuals with accents leads to discrimination against significant percentages of the population, many of whom belong to already marginalized groups. This paper looks specifically at the dialect of African American Vernacular English (AAVE), which is spoken by an estimated 80% of African Americans in the United States (Lippi-Green, 1997) or about 35-40 million people.

A major cause of the bias against AAVE is the lack of examples of this dialect in major speech corpora. The TIMIT dataset is the most popular speech corpus offered by the Linguistic Data Consortium and is often used for training and benchmarking speech recognition systems. It does not specifically provide statistics for AAVE speakers, but of the 630 speakers, only 26 (4%) are black, compared to the 538 (85%) who are white (Garofolo et al., 1993). Switchboard 1, another of the most commonly-used speech datasets, does provide a list of included dialects, yet AAVE is not among them (Godfrey and Holliman, 1993). A model which is trained on biased data will result in uneven performance.

Despite this bias against AAVE in many ASR systems, there has been very little scholarship either identifying this issue or proposing solutions. A number of popular press articles have called attention to the challenges faced by speakers with accents attempting to use products such as Amazon Alexa (Paul, 2017) or Google Assistant (Harwell, 2018), but there is a gap in the academic literature on AAVE in ASR, which this paper aims to fill.

Many papers have been published related to ASR systems for under-resourced dialects in English and other languages, using a variety of techniques. (Cucu et al., 2012) apply the technique of statistical machine translation to Romanian. (Elmahdy et al., 2013) and (Lehr et al., 2014) use transfer learning to adapt ASR systems trained on news corpora to under-resourced dialects. Using a sequence-to-sequence model, (Li et al., 2018)

Proceedings of the Student Research Workshop associated with RANLP-2019, pages 16–20,
Varna, Bulgaria, Sep 2–4, 2019.
https://doi.org/10.26615/issn.2603-2821.2019_003

Description	SAE Example	AAVE Example
consonant cluster reduction	first office	firs' office
devoicing of final consonants	bad	bat
variation of interdental fricatives	the	da
r-lessness	forever	fo'eva
-ing endings	walking	walkin'

Table 1: Common Phonetic Features of African American Vernacular English (Kendall et al., 2018)

combine language and pronunciation models into a single neural network for transcribing a variety of English dialects. Comparing all of these methods, and the many others which have shown success, for AAVE is beyond the scope of this paper, though these are promising avenues for future research. This preliminary study takes the approach of training a dialect-specific model for AAVE and SAE, drawing from the approach of (Soto et al., 2016).

1.1 African American Vernacular English

AAVE is a dialect of English commonly spoken some or all of the time by black persons in the United States, many of whom code-switch. It goes by other names including African American Language, Black English, and Ebonics (Kendall et al., 2018). While there are regional variations within the dialect, the majority of the phonetic and grammatical traits remain common across regions. Table 1 enumerates a few of the common phonetic features of AAVE; grammatical features were left out as this study's focus is on pronunciation.

1.2 Standard American English

SAE is the baseline to which other dialects are compared to; speakers of this dialect are perceived to be speaking without an accent. It is the language taught in classrooms and that spoken by newscasters and those in formal settings (Kretzchmar Jr., 2008). Labov observed that individuals exhibit more of the features of SAE as they increase attention to their language, indicating that the features of SAE are generally known and agreed upon, whether or not speakers use them in everyday speech (Labov, 2012).

2 Methodology

2.1 Data

Both the AAVE and the SAE speech data came from the Corpus of Regional African American Language (CORAAL) published by the University of Oregon (Kendall and Farrington, 2018). This dataset consists of audio files and time-aligned transcripts of interviews between SAE-speaking interviewers and AAVE-speaking interviewees. A subset of speakers located in Washington D.C. was used, to minimize the effects of regional accents within the dialect.

There were forty-two speakers–six interviewers and thirty-six interviewees–and 31,468 utterances across the training and testing sets. All speakers were adults, ranging in age from eighteen to seventy-seven. The gender-split of the AAVE speakers was ten female and twenty-six male; the genders of the interviewers were not provided.

2.2 Preprocessing

All audio files were split into utterances by the timecodes given in the transcripts. Each utterance was of a single speaker and was an average of four seconds long. These audio files were converted to 16-bit 16kHz mono WAVE files. The transcripts were sanitized to remove punctuation, lowercase all letters, and expand numerals into words. Regex matching was used to remove instances of sound effects, pauses, and other non-verbal entities present in the transcripts.

2.3 Model Training

Recent advances in neural networks have shifted the state of the art away from the hidden Markov models previously common in the field. Neural network models, rather than being passed lists of possible words, iteratively learn to match the patterns of words and phonemes to their written equivalents. The tool used for training in the study is Mozilla's DeepSpeech (Hannun et al., 2014), which is built on recurrent neural networks. This tool was chosen for ease of use as well as its demonstrated performance on noisy environments and with high speaker variation.

An AAVE model was trained using just the data from the AAVE-speaking interviewees. An SAE

Utterance Dialect	Model Dialect	Word Error Rate	Levenshtein Distance
AAVE	Combined	1.1509	18.7501
AAVE	AAVE	0.9363	15.2848
AAVE	SAE	1.1886	21.1567
SAE	Combined	1.1254	15.0589
SAE	SAE	1.0413	12.9967
SAE	AAVE	1.0492	15.5483

Table 2: Error Rates by Dialect

Gold Standard: you know take care of hisself

AAVE Model: you know tay car sef

Combined Model: you know tha co sa

Figure 1: Model Outputs for an Example AAVE Utterance

model was similarly trained on data from only the interviewers. To provide a baseline during evaluation, a model was trained using a combined set of all the data. Additionally, the dialect models were tested on the opposite dialect's utterances to examine whether there were major differences in the difficulty of the two datasets contributing to the error rates and to simulate how a large model trained only on SAE data would perform. A 70-20-10 split was used for the training, dev, and test sets. The splits were done to ensure that all speakers had proportional representation in each of the sets. For AAVE, the training set had 15,857 utterances, the dev set had 4,467, and the test set had 2,266. The SAE training set had 6,199 utterances, the dev set had 1,783, and the test set had 902. There were an average of 6.2 words per utterance for AAVE and 4.6 words per utterance for SAE.

3 Results

Transcripts were generated by passing each utterance in the test set through the baseline combined model, the dialect-specific model corresponding to the dialect of the utterance, and the dialect-specific model of the other dialect. These outputs were then compared to the gold standard transcripts provided by CORAAL.

Accuracy of the transcripts was measured using both word error rate (WER) and Levenshtein distance. The WER is a measure of the number of full word matches between the output and the gold standard, as a percent of the word count. It

provides a good metric for judging the readability of the output, but the drawback of this measure is it does not allow for partial credit. The neural network based approach to building ASR models does not pass pre-defined word lists and often results in matches on certain phonemes within a word rather than the entire word. For instance, in the example output shown in Figure 1, both the AAVE-only and the combined model correctly matched "you know" but missed the other three words, resulting in equal WER scores. However, the AAVE model picked up on the "ar" sound in "care" and the "f" sound in "hisself", both of which the combined model incorrectly transcribed. In order to quantify this behavior, the Levenshtein distance was used, which is a measure of the number of character insertions, deletions, or substitutions needed to transform the output into the gold standard. For both WER and Levenshtein distance, a lower score indicates higher accuracy.

The hypothesis of the study was that the highest performance for each dialect's data would be from the same-dialect model and that the worst performance would result from running the opposite dialect's model. The results support this hypothesis, as Table 2 illustrates. In each section, the bottom row shows the performance when the utterance dialect is opposite that of the model. For both AAVE and SAE, this had the highest error rate as measured by the Levenshtein Distance. The middle row of each section, when the dialects were aligned between utterances and the model, the error rates were lowest for both WER and Levenshtein distance.

The WER rates are nearly all above 1 due to the outputs putting in extra word breaks. Though the overall accuracy is low, both the AAVE and the SAE models significantly improved accuracy over the baseline combined model for WER and Levenshtein Distance. Table 3 shows the percent improvement over the combined-dialect baseline for the two dialect models for both accuracy measures. The improvement for the AAVE model was over 18% when using the Levenshtein Distance to provide a character-level error rate. There was a larger increase for the AAVE utterances, likely due to the higher number of utterances for that dialect as well as the utterances being longer. Many of the SAE utterances were short interjections such as "I see" and "mm hm".

Dialect	WER	Levenshtein Distance
AAVE	16.6%	18.5%
SAE	7.5%	13.7%

Table 3: Improvements in Error Rate Between Dialect-Specific Model and Combined Model

4 Conclusions and Future Work

Different dialects or accents within the same language can have conflicting patterns of phonemes. An automatic voice recognition tool which tries to handle all dialects with the same model is setting itself up for challenges. The ambiguities arising from having to learn opposing patterns can cause errors and lower overall accuracy. If the model does not handle these ambiguities, whatever pattern was seen more in the training data could win out, causing a bias against dialects with lower representation. Frequently, the majority dialect in training sets is Standard English. Those who do not speak Standard English, such as speakers of African American Vernacular English, are more often misunderstood. This study shows the potential of using dialect-specific models to remedy this situation.

Applications which handle diverse speech can benefit from using dialect-specific models for speech recognition. This is particularly useful in contexts where the speech data is gathered in advance, rather than in real-time. In this case, the increase in transcription accuracy would outweigh the small increase in processing time to classify the dialect of the speech.

Future directions for this research are growing the AAVE dataset used for training to improve the overall accuracy of the model and expanding to other dialects. A classifier could also be trained to automatically select the appropriate model for a given utterance to remove the preprocessing step of manually separating the utterances by dialect before passing them to the speech-to-text models.

Additionally, transfer learning techniques could be explored as a comparison to the dialect-specific method explored in this study.

References

Horia Cucu, Laurent Besacier, Corneliu Burileanu, and Andi Buzo. 2012. Asr domain adaptation methods for low-resourced languages: Application to romanian language. In *20th European Signal Processing Conference*. pages 1648–1652.

Mohamed Elmahdy, Mark Hasegawa-Johnson, and Eiman Mustafawi. 2013. A transfer learning approach for under-resourced arabic dialects speech recognition. In *Workshop on Less Resourced Languages, new technologies, new challenges and opportunities (LTC 2013)*. pages 60–64.

John S. Garofolo, Lori F. Lamel, William M. Fisher, Jonathan G. Fiscus, David S. Pallett, Nancy L. Dahlgren, and Victor Zue. 1993. Timit acoustic-phonetic continuous speech corpus ldc93s1. *Linguistic Data Consortium* https://catalog.ldc.upenn.edu/docs/LDC93S1.

John Godfrey and Edward Holliman. 1993. Switchboard-1 release 2 ldc97s62. *Linguistic Data Consortium* https://catalog.ldc.upenn.edu/LDC97S62.

Awni Hannun, Carl Case, Jared Casper, Bryan Catanzaro, Greg Diamos, Erich Elsen, Ryan Prenger, Sanjeev Satheesh, Shubho Sengupta, Adam Coates, and Andrew Y. Ng. 2014. Deep speech: Scaling up end-to-end speech recognition https://arxiv.org/abs/1412.5567.

Drew Harwell. 2018. The accent gap. *The Washington Post* .

Tyler Kendall and Charlie Farrington. 2018. The corpus of regional african american language. *The Online Resources for African American Language Project* (2018.10.06). http://oraal.uoregon.edu/coraal.

Tyler Kendall, Jason McLarty, and Brooke Josler. 2018. Oraal: Online resources for african american language: Aal facts. *The Online Resources for African American Language Project* https://oraal.uoregon.edu/facts.

William A. Kretzchmar Jr. 2008. Standard american english pronunciation. In *Varieties of English 2: The Americas and the Caribbean*, pages 37–51.

William Labov. 2012. *Dialect Diversity in America*, University of Virginia Press, chapter A Hidden Consensus, pages 9–10.

Maider Lehr, Kyle Gorman, and Izhak Shafran. 2014. Discriminative pronunciation modeling for dialectal speech recognition. *INTERSPEECH 2014* .

Bo Li, Tara N. Sainath, Khe Chai Sim, Michiel Bacchiani, Eugene Weinstein, Patrick Nguyen, Zhifeng Chen, Yonghui Wu, and Kanishka Rao. 2018. Multi-dialect speech recognition with a single sequence-to-sequence model. In *IEEE International Conference on Acoustics, Speech, and Signal Processing*. pages 4749–4753.

Rosina Lippi-Green. 1997. What we talk about when we talk about ebonics: Why definitions matter. *The Black Scholar* (27.2).

Sonia Paul. 2017. Voice is the next big platform, unless you have an accent. *Wired* .

Victor Soto, Olivier Siohan, Mohamed Elfeky, and Pedro Moreno. 2016. Selection and combination of hypotheses for dialectal speech recognition. *2016 IEEE International Conference on Acoustics, Speech and Signal Processing (ICASSP)* .

Rachael Tatman and Conner Kasten. 2017. Gender and dialect bias in youtube's automatic captions. In *Proceedings of the First ACL Workshop on Ethics in Natural Language Processing*. Association for Computational Linguistics, pages 53–59. https://doi.org/10.18653/v1/W17-1606.

W. Xiong, L. Wu, F. Alleva, J. Droppo, X. Huang, and A. Stolcke. 2017. The microsoft 2017 conversational speech recognition system. *Microsoft AI and Research Technical Report MSR-TR-2017-39* https://arxiv.org/pdf/1708.06073.pdf.

Multilingual Language Models
for Named Entity Recognition in German and English

Antonia Baumann
Trinity College Dublin
Dublin 2, Ireland
abaumann@tcd.ie

Abstract

We assess the language specificity of recent language models by exploring the potential of a multilingual language model. In particular, we evaluate Google's multilingual BERT (mBERT) model on Named Entity Recognition (NER) in German and English. We expand the work on language model fine-tuning by Howard and Ruder (2018), applying it to the BERT architecture.

We successfully reproduce the NER results published by Devlin et al. (2019). Our results show that the multilingual language model generalises well for NER in the chosen languages, matching the native model in English and comparing well with recent approaches for German. However, it does not benefit from the added fine-tuning methods.

1 Introduction

Language modelling (LM) has proven to improve many natural language processing (NLP) tasks across a wide set of tasks and domains (Dai and Le, 2015; Peters et al., 2018; Radford et al., 2018; Ruder, 2016; Devlin et al., 2019). These language models encompass the requirements "for natural language understanding technology to be maximally useful" generalising to multiple tasks, genres and datasets (Wang et al., 2018).

We argue that language models could also generalise along the language axis. Cross-lingual language understanding (XLU) significantly increases the usability of language technologies for international products such as Word, Facebook, or Google (all utilising varying levels NLP, for example translation, autocompletion or grammar correction). This interest is supported by Conneau et al. (2018) from Facebook AI[1], who laid one of the first milestones by creating a multilingual natural language inference corpus (XNLI) for XLU evaluation.

Therefore, our first research aim is to investigate the cross-lingual potential of Google's multilingual BERT (mBERT). Our experiments aim to establish a baseline under good transfer learning conditions: closely related languages with enough native data for fine-tuning. We expand the baselines Google published on natural lanugage inference (NLI) to named entity recognition (NER).

The second aim is to analyse if the BERT architecture benefits from special fine-tuning methods proposed by Howard and Ruder (2018). These showed significant performance increase for an LSTM-based architecture, but have not been generalised to other architectures. Besides LSTMs, Transformers are becoming an increasingly popular choice for language models, making BERT an ideal candidate to incorporate these fine-tuning methods.

Contributions: We make the following contributions to current LM research:

- We validate the original results published by Devlin et al. (2019), by replicating their NER experiment in Pytorch. For this we compare the method outlined in their paper and other replication attempts.

- We show that for NER, Google's multilingual BERT model matches the monolingual BERT model for English, and for German compares with most of the recent native models.

- We adapt the fine-tuning methods by Howard and Ruder (2018) for Google's BERT model. Our results show that slanted triangular learning rates improve the model, but gradual

---

[1] in collaboration with New York University

21

Proceedings of the Student Research Workshop associated with RANLP-2019, pages 21–27,
Varna, Bulgaria, Sep 2–4, 2019.
https://doi.org/10.26615/issn.2603-2821.2019_004

unfreezing and discriminative learning rates have no effect.

2 Related Work

There is a vast amount of pre-trained language model research. We briefly review the ones that this paper directly builds on.

2.1 Language Models

Bengio et al. (2003) published the first neural language model in 2003. Their basic architecture of (a) Embedding, (b) Encoding and (c) Pooling layer(s) is still used by neural language and word embedding models today. [2]

With the rise of recurrent neural networks (RNNs) in NLP, they became a better choice for (b) the Encoding layer of the LM (Mikolov et al., 2010). Especially the variation of a long-short-term memory (LSTM) RNN (Jozefowicz et al., 2016) which are still used by recent papers like Howard and Ruder (2018) and Peters et al. (2018). By combining a forward LM and a backward LM Peters et al. (2018) created a bidirectional language model (biLM).

Overall, the widely successful approach for language models is to (1) pre-train the LM on general text to predict the next sentence.[3] Then this language knowledge is transferred by (2) fine-tuning the model for the target task (Devlin et al., 2019; Howard and Ruder, 2018; Peters et al., 2018; Radford et al., 2018). The target tasks range from sentiment analysis in the movie domain (Howard and Ruder, 2018); named entity recognition for newspaper articles (Devlin et al., 2019); to question answering on Wikipedia data (Devlin et al., 2019; Peters et al., 2018; Radford et al., 2018).

2.2 Universal Language Model Fine-Tuning

Howard and Ruder (2018) introduced special LM fine-tuning methods, including a further step in between (1.5) where the language model is fine-tuned on the unlabelled task data using the language modelling objective.

In addition, they propose three more methods: Slanted triangular learning rates, an adaptation of the cyclic learning rates by Smith (2017, 2018). An individual learning rate for each layer (Discriminative learning); and gradual unfreezing where layers are slowly added to the training pool. Howard and Ruder (2018) found that the combination of all these additions worked best, reducing error rates by 18-24% on 6 text classification sets.

2.3 BERT

At the end of 2018, Google's BERT was the best performing model for the GLUE Benchmark[4] (Devlin et al., 2019; Wang et al., 2018). In contrast to previous language models they utilise a deeply bidirectional architecture for their transformer; meaning the model receives the whole sentence (or sentence pair) as input and each cell depends on the context of the previous and subsequent word in the sequence.

Due to this, BERT's training differs from other language models. The non-sequential input makes the next-word prediction task impossible. Instead, Devlin et al. (2019) train the model to predict masked words in the input sentence. For further cross-sentence context, they also trained it to classify if two sentences follow each other.

They argue that the added context improves the model, making more suited for sentence level tasks (Devlin et al., 2019). This is supported by their results on the tasks in the GLUE Benchmark, overall achieving an absolute improvement of 7.7%.

2.4 Multilingual Language Models

Out of the established language model architecture, BERT is the only one that also provides multilingual versions on their repository.[5] The mBERT model has been pre-trained on Wikipedia text from the top 104 languages. They evaluated their multilingual model on the cross-lingual natural language inference dataset (XNLI), showing good performance for the 6 languages they reported on (Conneau et al., 2018).

3 Multilingual BERT for NER

We use the multilingual BERT as our pre-trained LM. To evaluate its cross-lingual potential we select a task and multiple language for the experiments.

---

[2]Retrieved May 20th, 2019, from `http://ruder.io/word-embeddings-1/index.html#classicneurallanguagemodel`

[3]This is the most common language modelling objective.

[4]Retrieved May 20th, 2019, from `https://gluebenchmark.com/`

[5]Retrieved May 20th, 2019, from `https://github.com/google-research/bert`

3.1 Dataset & Languages

The CoNLL 2003 NER task (Tjong Kim Sang and De Meulder, 2003) was used by Devlin et al. (2019) to evaluate the English BERT model on NER. Since it also provides German data, it was the ideal candidate to validate our re-implementation of the model, evaluate the performance of the multilingual model on multiple languages, and compare against the monolingual model. The dataset is widely used for German NER and provides a baseline evaluation for the German model, that can be expanded to more recent datasets such as GermEval 2014 (Benikova et al., 2014).

The CoNLL dataset has been used with two different annotation types: IOB1 (described in the original paper (Tjong Kim Sang and De Meulder, 2003)) and BIO.[6] Since the BERT paper itself uses both annotation types in the examples they provide, it is unclear which one they used (Devlin et al., 2019). Our experiments compare the results of both annotation types.

3.2 Method/Architecture

The overall structure of the NER experiments is abstracted in figure 1. It shows that all experiments only differ in the data pre-processing and BERT model selected.

We follow the same structure outlined in the BERT paper: The data is pre-processed using Google's WordPiece tokenization, and then converted into a BERT input feature consisting of token ids, segment mask and attention mask. A tokenoptimal one classification layer[7] is added to convert the BERT output into label probabilities over the set of annotations. We use the softmax cross-entropy loss and the standard hyperparameter optimisation for BERT.[8]

We evaluate the model using the F1 score following the original CoNLL 2003 shared task (Tjong Kim Sang and De Meulder, 2003).

3.3 Adaptation of Fine-Tuning Methods

Howard and Ruder (2018) described their fine-tuning methods for their 4-layer LSTM. This sections described our adaptations to apply them to BERT, a 12-layer transformer.

---

[6]Also called IOB2.

[7]Linear classification layer

[8]Linear learning rate warmup.

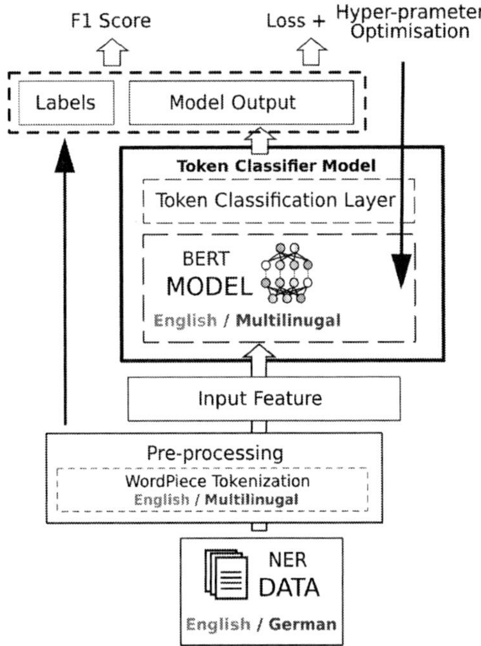

Figure 1: NER model architecture

Slanted Triangular Learning Rates This fine-tuning method is already used by BERT, however, Devlin et al. (2019) call it linear warmup. Therefore, we do not need to adapt this method, instead we compare BERT's performance with and without.

Discriminative Fine-Tuning Howard and Ruder (2018) used the following formula to calculate the learning rate for each layer:

$$\eta^n = \frac{\eta^0}{\delta^n} \tag{1}$$

where η^0, the learning rate of the top layer is manually selected. They empirically found a $\delta = 2.6$ to work well for their model. In the most recent ULMFiT implementation taught by Howard in his new course[9] η^0, on the other hand, decreases after every epoch.

Since a δ of 2.6 would lead to minuscule learning rates for the lower levels for BERT, we compare δ values: 2.6, 1.6 and $1^{[10]}$. Further, we measure several η^0's for each epoch to find the most optimal one.

---

[9]Retrieved May 20th, 2019, from `https://nbviewer.jupyter.org/github/fastai/course-v3/blob/master/nbs/dl1/lesson3-imdb.ipynb`

[10]Meaning a constant learning rate for all layers.

Gradual Unfreezing The difference in layer count also affects the unfreezing procedure. Going from top to bottom, Howard and Ruder (2018) added a single layer to the set of trained layers after each epoch, resulting in 4 epochs of fine-tuning.

Applying the same procedure to BERT would lead to 12 epochs, which is 3 to 4 times as much as the standard BERT task fine-tuning of 3-4 epochs. Instead we unfreeze the layers in groups of 3, thus, fine-tuning the model for 5 epochs.

4 Experiments

This section discusses the results of the NER experiments.

hyperparameter	options
batch size	16, 32
learning rate	2e-5, 3e-5, 5e-5
epochs	3,4

Table 1: BERT fine-tuning hyperparameters

4.1 Replication of English Results

For the replication, we performed a grid search over the hyperparameter options listed by Devlin et al. (2019) (see Table 1) and evaluate them on the development set. The best parameters[11] were then used to evaluate on the test set.

Table 2 shows that our implementation of $BERT_{BASE}$ for NER matches the original for the IOB1 annotation style. Therefore, validating the original results and our re-implementation. We use the same structure for the multilingual experiments.

---

[11]Batch size: 16; learning rate: 3e-5; epochs: 4

System	Annot.	Dev	Test
$BERT_{LARGE}$	-	96.6	92.8
$BERT_{BASE}$	-	96.4	92.4
our $BERT_{BASE}$	IOB1	96.4	**92.6**
	BIO	95.9	92.2
Multilingual BERT	IOB1	96.4	91.9
	BIO	**96.5**	92.1

Table 2: [English Data] BERT model F1 results, compared to original paper. All results recorded are averaged out of 5 randomly initialised runs.

System	Annot.	Dev	Test
Ahmed & Mehler	IOB1	-	83.64
Riedl & Pado	-	-	84.73
Akbik et al. (2018)	-	-	**88.33**
Multilingual BERT	IOB1	**88.44**	85.81
	BIO	87.49	84.98

Table 3: [German Data] F1 Score evaluation on German CoNLL-2003 data, development and test set. Comparing our results with the state-of-the-art native models.

4.1.1 Multilingual BERT

We evaluate the multilingual BERT model on both the German and English dataset.

German We compare our results for the German data against the most recent state-of-the-art: for example Ahmed and Mehler (2018) used a Long-Short-Term Memory (LSTM) model with a Conditional Random Field (CRF) on top. Riedl and Padó (2018) lead with their bidirectional LSTM, which has been pre-trained on GermEval NER data.

As seen in Table 3 the multilingual model outperforms these first two models; notably for IOB1 annotation, and slightly exceeding Riedl and Padó (2018) with BIO. Riedl and Padó (2018) pre-trained on German data and fine-tuned for 15 epochs, in contrast to our multilingual pre-training and 3 epochs of fine-tuning.

The most recent and leading approach by Akbik et al. (2018), uses an LSTM + CRF with their novel contextual string embeddings [12] concatenated with Glove embeddings (Pennington et al., 2014), and task-trained character features. The contextual string embeddings were trained on half a million German words.

Using only these proposed contextual string embeddings, their models achieves 85.78 for F1 on the CoNLL dataset, similar to our multilingual model. Their research shows that the embeddings chosen strongly influences the models performance. We find that further comparison and analysis is needed to see how the multilingual model might benefit from concatenating multiple embeddings.

Overall, the multilingual Bert model compares well against the current state-of-the-art given that it is the only model using non-native embeddings.

---

[12]Forward + Backward character embeddings

Model	Optim	Epoch 3		Epoch 4	
English BERT	with BertAdam	96.31	$\pm$ 0.13	96.42	$\pm$ 0.09
	without BertAdam	95.76	$\pm$ 0.47	94.80	$\pm$ 2.39
Multilingual BERT	with BertAdam	96.51	$\pm$ 0.18	96.55	$\pm$ 0.21
(English)	without BertAdam	95.88	$\pm$ 0.74	96.25	$\pm$ 0.06
Multilingual BERT	with BertAdam	88.44	$\pm$ 0.35	88.23	$\pm$ 0.46
(German)	without BertAdam	86.69	$\pm$ 1.12	85.24	$\pm$ 2.17

Table 4: Comparing the multilingual/English model with and without the BertAdam optimiser using the learning rate warmup. The scores reported are on the development set (IBO1). The optimal hyperparameters from the previous section were used for each model. Scores are averaged out of 4 random initialised runs.

The results by Akbik et al. (2018) show that our LM could be improved through richer embeddings

English Table 2 shows that the multilingual model matches the native for the development scores, yet it does not generalise as well to the test set.

4.2 Additional Fine-Tuning

First, we analyse the effect of the linear learning rate warmup: the results in Table 4 show that the warmup improves the scores and their stability.

Second, the other fine-tuning methods are added to the task fine-tuning step. For each layer the best discriminative learning rate is selected, from a set of manually selected η^0 values and the varying δ.

We measure the effectiveness of the additional LM fine-tuning on the target data by comparing (1) the "plain" BERT for task fine-tuning, (2) adding the additional fine-tuning methods and (3) adding the LM fine-tuning for 10/20 epochs.

The results in tables 5 and 6 show that the added fine-tuning methods do not exhibit any improvement over the "plain" BERT model. Further, there is no significant difference when adding the extra LM fine-tuning.

Our adaptation of the fine-tuning methods, however, are not fine-grained enough to allow for more detailed analysis. Compared to the multilingual model, the quick conversion does not yield results, instead a more in-depth approach is required to identify how a transformer is affected by these methods.

5 Conclusion

Pre-trained language models have led to significant empirical improvements for English natu-

English BERT	Dev	Test
Plain	**96.4**	**92.6**
+ Task fine-tuning	95.60	92.38
+ 10e LM & Task fine-tuning	95.58	92.42
+ 20e LM & Task fine-tuning	95.91	92.36

Table 5: English BERT fine-tuning F1 results. Averaged over 2 runs.

Multilingual BERT	Dev	Test
Plain	**88.44**	**85.81**
+ Task fine-tuning	87.50	85.78
+ 10e LM & Task fine-tuning	87.11	84.98
+ 20e LM & Task fine-tuning	87.93	85.16

Table 6: Multilingual BERT fine-tuning F1 results for German. Averaged over 2 runs.

ral language understanding. We validate parts of those findings by replicating the BERT result for NER.

Further, our work demonstrates that the expansion to cross-lingual language models holds a lot of potential. For German we outperform most recent models, leaving some room for improvement. The English the multilingual model closely matched the native one, in contrast to the BERT results reported for the XNLI task, where the English model noticeably outperformed the multilingual one.[13]

The investigation into LM fine-tuning methods proposed by Howard and Ruder (2018) showed that they do not improve the BERT model, with exception of slanted triangular learning rates that

---

[13]Retrieved May 20th, 2019, from `https://github.com/google-research/bert`

are already used by BERT.

5.1 Future Work

Our experiments support the hypothesis of cross-lingual language models for general NLP. The improvements Akbik et al. (2018) achieved with their embedding work, should be used on language models; to evaluate if they provide a similar benefit, not only for NER but general NLP tasks.

In the future, this should be expanded to more tasks and languages. Such as Wu and Dredze (2019), who concurrent to our work showed mBERT's zero-shot transfer learning potential.

Possible areas of focus are morphologically complex languages such as Finish, Korean and Tamil [14] since typological properties of languages can impact "language-agnostic" models (Gerz et al., 2018).

Further, Lample and Conneau (2019) show that cross-lingual language models can be improved on by cross-lingual language model (XLM) pre-training.

Acknowledgments

I would like to thank my supervisor Alfredo Maldonado for his consistent support and guidance throughout the project. His expertise and focus really helped to shape this work. Further, I would like to thank him for the encouragement and support in submitting this student research paper.

The research in this paper was supported by the ADAPT Centre for Digital Content Technology (https://www.adaptcentre.ie), funded under the SFI Research Centres Programme (Grant 13/RC/2106) and is co-funded under the European Regional Development Fund.

References

Sajawel Ahmed and Alexander Mehler. 2018. Resource-size matters: Improving neural named entity recognition with optimized large corpora. In *2018 17th IEEE International Conference on Machine Learning and Applications (ICMLA)*. IEEE, pages 919–924.

Alan Akbik, Duncan Blythe, and Roland Vollgraf. 2018. Contextual string embeddings for sequence labeling. In *Proceedings of the 27th International Conference on Computational Linguistics*. Association for Computational Linguistics, Santa Fe, New Mexico, USA, pages 1638–1649. https://www.aclweb.org/anthology/C18-1139.

Yoshua Bengio, Réjean Ducharme, Pascal Vincent, and Christian Jauvin. 2003. A neural probabilistic language model. *Journal of machine learning research* 3(Feb):1137–1155.

Darina Benikova, Chris Biemann, Max Kisselew, and Sebastian Pado. 2014. Germeval 2014 named entity recognition shared task: companion paper .

Alexis Conneau, Ruty Rinott, Guillaume Lample, Adina Williams, Samuel Bowman, Holger Schwenk, and Veselin Stoyanov. 2018. XNLI: Evaluating cross-lingual sentence representations. In *Proceedings of the 2018 Conference on Empirical Methods in Natural Language Processing*. pages 2475–2485.

Andrew M Dai and Quoc V Le. 2015. Semi-supervised sequence learning. In *Advances in neural information processing systems*. pages 3079–3087.

Jacob Devlin, Ming-Wei Chang, Kenton Lee, and Kristina Toutanova. 2019. BERT: Pre-training of deep bidirectional transformers for language understanding. In *Proceedings of the 2019 Conference of the North American Chapter of the Association for Computational Linguistics: Human Language Technologies, Volume 1 (Long and Short Papers)*. pages 4171–4186.

Daniela Gerz, Ivan Vulić, Edoardo Maria Ponti, Roi Reichart, and Anna Korhonen. 2018. On the relation between linguistic typology and (limitations of) multilingual language modeling. In *Proceedings of the 2018 Conference on Empirical Methods in Natural Language Processing*. pages 316–327.

Jeremy Howard and Sebastian Ruder. 2018. Universal language model fine-tuning for text classification. In *Proceedings of the 56th Annual Meeting of the Association for Computational Linguistics (Volume 1: Long Papers)*. pages 328–339.

Rafal Jozefowicz, Oriol Vinyals, Mike Schuster, Noam Shazeer, and Yonghui Wu. 2016. Exploring the limits of language modeling. *arXiv preprint arXiv:1602.02410* .

Guillaume Lample and Alexis Conneau. 2019. Cross-lingual language model pretraining. *arXiv preprint arXiv:1901.07291* .

Tomáš Mikolov, Martin Karafiát, Lukáš Burget, Jan Černocký, and Sanjeev Khudanpur. 2010. Recurrent neural network based language model. In *Eleventh annual conference of the international speech communication association*.

Jeffrey Pennington, Richard Socher, and Christopher Manning. 2014. Glove: Global vectors for word representation. In *Proceedings of the 2014 conference on empirical methods in natural language processing (EMNLP)*. pages 1532–1543.

Matthew Peters, Mark Neumann, Mohit Iyyer, Matt Gardner, Christopher Clark, Kenton Lee, and Luke

---

[14] All included in mBERT's pre-training data

Zettlemoyer. 2018. Deep contextualized word representations. In *Proceedings of the 2018 Conference of the North American Chapter of the Association for Computational Linguistics: Human Language Technologies, Volume 1 (Long Papers)*. Association for Computational Linguistics, New Orleans, Louisiana, pages 2227–2237. https://doi.org/10.18653/v1/N18-1202.

Alec Radford, Karthik Narasimhan, Tim Salimans, and Ilya Sutskever. 2018. Improving language understanding by generative pre-training. *URLhttps://s3-us-west-2.amazonaws. com/openai-assets/research-covers/ languageunsupervised/ languageunderstandingpaper.pdf*
.

Martin Riedl and Sebastian Padó. 2018. A named entity recognition shootout for german. In *Proceedings of the 56th Annual Meeting of the Association for Computational Linguistics (Volume 2: Short Papers)*. pages 120–125.

Sebastian Ruder. 2016. An overview of gradient descent optimization algorithms. *arXiv preprint arXiv:1609.04747* .

Leslie N Smith. 2017. Cyclical learning rates for training neural networks. In *2017 IEEE Winter Conference on Applications of Computer Vision (WACV)*. IEEE, pages 464–472.

Leslie N Smith. 2018. A disciplined approach to neural network hyper-parameters: Part 1–learning rate, batch size, momentum, and weight decay. *arXiv preprint arXiv:1803.09820* .

Erik F. Tjong Kim Sang and Fien De Meulder. 2003. Introduction to the conll-2003 shared task: Language-independent named entity recognition. In *Proceedings of the Seventh Conference on Natural Language Learning at HLT-NAACL 2003 - Volume 4*. Association for Computational Linguistics, Stroudsburg, PA, USA, CONLL '03, pages 142–147. https://doi.org/10.3115/1119176.1119195.

Alex Wang, Amanpreet Singh, Julian Michael, Felix Hill, Omer Levy, and Samuel Bowman. 2018. GLUE: A multi-task benchmark and analysis platform for natural language understanding. In *Proceedings of the 2018 EMNLP Workshop BlackboxNLP: Analyzing and Interpreting Neural Networks for NLP*. Association for Computational Linguistics, Brussels, Belgium, pages 353–355.

Shijie Wu and Mark Dredze. 2019. Beto, bentz, becas: The surprising cross-lingual effectiveness of bert. *arXiv preprint arXiv:1904.09077* .

Parts of Speech Tagging for Kannada

Swaroop L R, Rakshit Gowda G S, Shriram Hegde and Sourabh U
Department of Information Science and Engineering, Ramaiah Institute of Technology
{swarooplr13, rakshugs, usourabh2011, sshegde66}@gmail.com

Abstract

Parts of speech (POS) tagging is the process of assigning the part of speech tag to each and every word in a sentence. In this paper, we have presented POS tagger for Kannada, a low resource south Asian language, using Condition Random Fields. POS tagger developed in the work uses novel features native to Kannada language. The novel features include Sandhi splitting, where a compound word is broken down into two or more meaningful constituent words. The proposed model is trained and tested on the tagged dataset which contains 21 thousand sentences and achieves a highest accuracy of 94.56%.

1 Introduction

Kannada, an Asian language spoken in southern part of India, is highly agglutinative and rich in derivational morphology. The language has about 2000 years of history and is one of the top 40 most spoken languages of the world. Kannada has clear standards characterized for each part of its structure. Even though Kannada is a Dravidian Language, with time Kannada has been influenced significantly by Sanskrit.

In Kannada, Sandhi is the process where two or more words join based on certain Sandhi rules to form a compound word. During the process of Sandhi, formation changes occur at the word boundaries. For example,

ನಾವು (navu) + ಎಲ್ಲ (yella) = ನಾವೆಲ್ಲ (navella)

ಗಾಳಿ (gaali) + ಅನ್ನು (annu) = ಗಾಳಿಯನ್ನು (gaaliyannu)

Kannada adopts all the Sandhi rules defined in Sanskrit and has three additional Sandhi rules. A Sandhi splitter isolates the constituent words of a Sandhi word utilizing an extensive lexicon and Sandhi rules. Sandhi splitting of a compound word into its component words gives valuable information about its morphology and parts of speech of the compound word.

2 Literature Survey

POS tagging for Indian languages and especially for Dravidian Languages is a difficult task due to the unavailability of annotated data for these languages. Various techniques have been applied for POS tagging in Indian languages.

Gadde et al. (2018) used morphological features with TNT HMM tagger Brants et al (2000) and obtained 92.36% for Hindi and 91.23 % in Telugu. The Hindi POS tagger used Hindi Treebank of size 450K. Ekbal et al. (2008) used SVM for POS tagging in Bengali obtaining 86% accuracy. A semi-supervised pattern-based bootstrapping technique was implemented by Ganesh et al. (2014) to build a Tamil POS Tagger. Their system scored 87.74% accuracy on 20000 documents containing 271K unique words.

Very little work has been done on Kannada because of scarcity of quality annotated data. Antony et al. (2010) was the initial paper which presented part-of-speech tagger for Kannada. They have proposed a tag set consisting of 30 tags. The tag set comprises 5 tags for nouns, 1 tag for pronoun, 8 tags for verbs, 3 for punctuation, two for numbers and 1 each for adjective, adverb, conjunction, echo, reduplication, intensifier, postposition, emphasize, determiner, complementizer, and question word. The researchers have used Support Vector Classification (SVC) a variation of Support Vector Machine (SVM) used for classification problems and tested on 56,000 words for which they obtained an accuracy of 86%.

Proceedings of the Student Research Workshop associated with RANLP-2019, pages 28–31,
Varna, Bulgaria, Sep 2–4, 2019.
https://doi.org/10.26615/issn.2603-2821.2019_005

The POS tagger tool using Hidden Markov Model (HMM) for Telugu is developed and tested on Kannada Corpus by Siva Reddy et al. (2011). The model gave the F-measure of 77.63 and 77.66 for cross-language and mono-lingual taggers respectively.

Shambhavi et al. (2012) worked on POS tagging for Kannada using Maximum Entropy approach. For training the POS tagger, 51267 words were tagged manually with the help of the tagset. The tagset consisted of 25 tags and the words were collected from EMILLE corpus. Also, Shambhavi et al. (2012) reported 79.9% and 84.58% accuracy using second order HMM and CRF.A POS Tagger for Kannada Sentence Translation is done by Mallamma et al. (2012). Decision trees are used to tag the words.

Prathyusha et al. (2016) a rule based Agama Sandhi splitter has been presented. Agama Sandhi is one of the 7 Sandhis in Kannada language. M. R. Shree et al. (2016) adopted a CRF model for Sandhi splitting. The output of the model is a character level split of the word, hence constituent meaningful base words of the compound (Sandhi) word can't be identified.
AN Akshatha et al. (2017) developed a rule based Sandhi splitter to extract component words from a compound (Sandhi) word.

3   Methodologies

This section gives a description of the dataset used, the features utilized to train the conditional random fields model.

3.1   Dataset

We use the Kannada Treebank project dataset to train our POS tagger. The Kannada Treebank contains three corpora divided based on topic as General, Conversational, and Tourism. The data set is available on the website[1].

---

[1] *https://ltrc.iiit.ac.in/showfile.php?filename=downloads/kolhi/*

Topic	Tokens	Sentences
General	218,530	17,175
Tourism	26,521	1,883
Conversational	26,521	2,260

Table 1: Corpus information

The corpora were tagged using the Unified Parts of Speech (POS) Standard in Indian Languages drafted by the Department of Information Technology, Govt. of India.

3.2   Models

Two different CRF models were developed in this work. The features used in the first model [Model 1] are:
1.   **Context:** The word to be tagged, its preceding three words and succeeding three words
2.   **Length:** A binary feature with a value of 0 if the word is shorter than three characters, value of 1 otherwise
3.   **Ending characters** (suffix): Last three characters of word.
4.   **Is Punctuation**: A binary feature with value 1 if the token contains a non-alphanumeric character and zero otherwise
5.   **Is Digit**: A binary feature with a value of 1 if the token contained a digit and 0 otherwise.
6.   **POS of first Sandi word**: It is a novel feature where a compound (Sandhi) word is split into its component words, the parts of speech of the first component word is provided as feature value. In case the word is not a Sandhi word i.e. a non compound word the POS tag of word in the word unigram model is provided as feature, if the POS tag is unavailable a none identifier is provide as feature value. For example the compound word ನಾವೆಲ್ಲ (navella meaning "all of us") is split into

ನಾವು ("navu" meaning "us") and ಎಲ್ಲ ("yella" meaning "all") the POS tag of "us" i.e. pronoun is the feature value.

A rule based Sandhi splitter described in AN Akshatha et al. (2017) was used to extract component words from a compound (Sandhi) word. The Sandhi word given as an input is scanned from the left to right to find the longest prefix. This longest prefix will be referred to as expected prefix. This expected prefix is removed from the Sandhi word leaving behind the Sandhi letters and expected suffix, referred to as remainder word. The last letter of the expected prefix is then removed from the expected prefix and added to the beginning of the remainder word. The first one or two letters of the remainder word is most likely to be containing the resultant Sandhi letters. These letters are looked up in the Sandhi rules to identify the Sandhi. Using the reverse Sandhi rule base, the Sandhi letters are replaced with the prefix's ending letter and suffix's beginning   letter according to the Sandhi rules. The expected prefix is then added to the remainder word and the words are split. The prefix and suffix thus generated are looked up in the dictionary containing root Kannada words . If both prefix and suffix are found, the Sandhi rule which was applied to split the words is the required Sandhi and the process is terminated as the Sandhi, prefix and suffix words are identified successfully. If the Sandhi is not determined, the second longest prefix is assigned as the expected prefix and the process   is continued until the Sandhi is determined or the expected prefix is null.

7. **Last component word**: The last component word of compound (Sandhi) word is used as feature, a none identifier is provided in case of a non-Sandhi word. For example, for the compound word ಹಣದಾಸೆ ("hanadase" meaning "desire for money") is split into ಹಣ ("hana" meaning "money") and ಆಸೆ ("aase" meaning "desire") the component "aase" is the feature value.

The second model [Model 2] uses all the above listed features along with word embedding feature.

8. **Word embedding**: The word embeddings are obtained by training the text corpus using the FastText tool Bojanowski et al., A. Joulin et al., E. Grave et al. Each word is represented by a vector of size 30. Word embeddings represent the current token at a higher level abstraction that helps to recognize the semantics of the token that are not observed in the training set.

4 Results

Table 2 and 3 summarized the results achieved using both the models. Each corpus (General, Tourism and Conversational) is split with a 70-30 ratio for training and testing the POS tagger. In addition all the three corpora were combined to obtain a mixed corpus, the sentences from the three corpora were randomly jumbled and divided into training and testing data.

Accuracy = (No of correctly tagged words) / (Total no of words);

	General	Tourism	Convers-ational	Combined
Model 1	93.42	93.11	91.61	92.69
Model 2	95.84	94.96	93.47	94.56

Table 2: Accuracies of each model

	Precision	Recall	F1-Score
Model 1	91.8	92	91.6
Model 2	93.78	93.21	93.4

Table 3: Detailed result for combined corpus

The accuracy for Model 2 (with word embedding feature) is on the higher side compared to model 1, likewise the cost of training in terms of time and processing for model 2 is higher compared to model 1. The lower accuracies of conversational corpus are a result of higher frequency of colloquial words which makes Sandhi splitting harder. The General corpus being the largest corpus achieves the highest accuracy. The result for combined corpus is almost equal to the three individual corpora; this asserts the models are nearly domain independent. Table [4] gives detailed scores for individual parts of speech tag for Model 1. In this work the Bureau of Indian Standards (BIS) Part Of Speech (POS) tagset prepared for Indian Languages by the POS Tag Standardization Committee of Department of Information Technology has been followed.

POS Tags (BIS)	Precision	Recall	F1-score
N__NN	0.905	0.967	0.935
N__NNP	0.887	0.557	0.684
QT__QTC	0.978	0.858	0.914
DM__DMD	0.981	0.966	0.974
V__VM__VF	0.962	0.969	0.966
RD__PUNC	0.991	0.999	0.995
PR__PRP	0.955	0.962	0.958
V__VM__VNF	0.881	0.890	0.886
JJ	0.780	0.829	0.804
RB	0.739	0.653	0.693
CC__CCD	0.909	0.969	0.938
V__VM__VINF	0.918	0.816	0.864
PSP	0.875	0.920	0.897
CC__CCS	0.860	0.805	0.831
RP__RPD	0.858	0.724	0.786
RD__SYM	0.987	0.924	0.954
QT__QTF	0.706	0.572	0.632
DM__DMQ	0.833	0.714	0.769
DM_DMI	0.776	0.864	0.817
RP__INTF	0.622	0.505	0.557
N__NST	0.835	0.773	0.803
PR__PRQ	0.795	0.837	0.815
RP_INTF	0.687	0.201	0.300
V__VM__VNG	0.853	0.615	0.708
DM__DMI	0.560	0.467	0.509
V__VM	0.000	0.000	0.000
N_NNV	0.667	0.050	0.093
QT__QTO	0.974	0.521	0.679
RP__NEG	0.818	0.818	0.818
V__VAUX	0.738	0.413	0.479
RP__INJ	1.000	0.567	0.723
PR__PRF	0.934	0.966	0.950
CC__CCS__UT	0.000	0.000	0.000
PR__PRI	1.000	0.278	0.435
NULL	0.000	0.000	0.000
PR_PRI	0.667	0.194	0.300
CC_CCS	0.000	0.000	0.000
RD__ECH	1.000	0.333	0.500
N__NN	0.000	0.000	0.000
PR__PRC	1.000	1.000	1.000

Table 4: Result for each POS Tags of Model1

References

Gadde P and Yeleti M.V. 2008. *Improving statistical pos tagging using linguistic feature for hindi and telugu.* Proceedings of ICON-2010 Tools Contest on Indian Language Dependency Parsing, ICON.

Brants T. 2000. *A statistical part-of-speech tagger.* Proceedings of the sixth conference on Applied natural language processing.

Ekbal A. and Bandyopadhyay S. 2008. *Part of speech tagging in bengali using support vector machine.* International Conference on Information Technology.

Ganesh, J, Parthasarathi R, Geetha T, Balaji J. 2014. *Pattern based bootstrapping technique for Tamil pos tagging.* Mining Intelligence and Knowledge Exploration.

Antony P.J and Soman K.P. 2010. *Kernel based Part of Speech Tagger for Kannada.* Proceedings of the Ninth International Conference on Machine Learning and Cybernetics, Qingdao.

Siva Reddy and Serge Sharoff. 2011. *Cross Language POS Taggers (and other Tools) for Indian Languages: An Experiment with Kannada using Telugu Resources.* Proceedings of IJCNLP workshop on Cross Lingual Information Access: Computational Linguistics and the Information Need of Multilingual Societies.

Shambhavi B R, RamakanthKumar P and Revanth. 2012. *Maximum Entropy Approach to Kannada Part Of Speech Tagging.* International Journal of Computer Applications.

Shambhavi B R and RamakanthKumar. 2012. *Kannada Part-Of-Speech Tagging with Probabilistic Classifiers.* International Journal of Computer Applications.

Mallamma V Reddy and Dr. M. Hanumanthappa. 2012. *POS Tagger for Kannada Sentence Translation.* International Journal of Emerging Trends & Technology in Computer Science (IJETTCS).

H. L. Shashirekha and K. S. Vanishree. 2016. *Rule based Kannada Agama Sandhi splitter.* International Conference on Advances in Computing, Communications and Informatics (ICACCI), Jaipur.

M. R. Shree, S. Lakshmi and Shambhavi B.R. 2016. *A novel approach to Sandhi splitting at character level for Kannada language.* International Conference on Computation System and Information Technology for Sustainable Solutions (CSITSS), Bangalore.

S. R. Murthy, A. N. Akshatha, C. G. Upadhyaya and P. R. Kumar. 2017. *Kannada spell checker with sandhi splitter.* International Conference on Advances in Computing, Communications and Informatics (ICACCI), Udupi, 2017.

P. Bojanowski*, E. Grave*, A. Joulin, T. Mikolov, *Enriching Word Vectors with Subword Information.*

A. Joulin, E. Grave, P. Bojanowski, T. Mikolov. *Bag of Tricks for Efficient Text Classification.*

A. Joulin, E. Grave, P. Bojanowski, M. Douze, H. Jégou, T. Mikolov. *FastText.zip: Compressing text classification models.*

Cross-Lingual Coreference: The Case of Bulgarian and English

Zara Kancheva
LMaKP
IICT-BAS
Sofia, Bulgaria
`zara@bultreebank.org`

Abstract

The paper presents several common approaches towards cross- and multi-lingual coreference resolution in a search of the most effective practices to be applied within the work on Bulgarian-English manual coreference annotation of a short story. The work aims at outlining the typology of the differences in the annotated parallel texts. The results of the research prove to be comparable with the tendencies observed in similar works on other Slavic languages and show surprising differences between the types of markables and their frequency in Bulgarian and English.

1 Introduction

Coreference tends to be a common subject of research nowadays due to its various NLP applications like text summarization, question answering, information extraction, machine translation, named entity recognition, etc. For the accomplishment of these applications many coreference annotated corpora have been built and a number of annotation schemes have been created.

Many recent investigations focus on the coreference resolution in parallel corpora or translated texts with multiple languages (major and less wide-spread) and thus face a number of challenges like choosing between automatic and manual annotation, between different genres and size of the data, guidelines, tools and methods for analysis.

In the current research, the original English[1] text and the translated Bulgarian version of "The Adventure of the Speckled Band" by Sir A.C. Doyle are taken as a starting point for finding cross-lingual coreference similarities and differences. For this task, OntoNotes guidelines have been adapted to accommodate for the specifics of

the two languages. Both texts have been manually annotated within WebAnno system. The manual approach to the coreference annotation would contribute to the future work on the automatic processing by improving the evaluation process as a gold annotation. The investigation will be used for facilitating the creation of a coreference resolver for Bulgarian.

The paper is structured as follows: the next section presents relevant related work; section 3 presents the dataset and the annotation process; section 4 illustrates the typology of the differences observed; section 5 shows directions for future work, and concludes the paper.

2 Related Work

One of the main methods for treating coreference in parallel texts is the projection. Formerly used for various purposes as POS tags projection (Yarowsky et al., 2001), dependency structures projection (Hwa et al., 2005) or semantic roles projection (Pado and Lapata, 2005), this approach proves effective also for projecting coreference chains.

The work of (Postolache et al., 2006) is based on that method and applied to coreference for the first time, using a parallel corpus, containing three parts of the English original and Romanian translation of the novel "1984". The researches focus only on noun phrases and do automatic word alignment with a Romanian-English aligner; they extract the corresponding referential expressions and transfer the English coreference chains to Romanian.

(Grishina and Stede, 2015) apply knowledge-lean projection of coreference chains across three languages – English, German and Russian. In this research the specifics of the genre are also considered and thus argumentative newspaper articles,

---

[1]In the text we refer to English as a source language and to Bulgarian as a target one.

Proceedings of the Student Research Workshop associated with RANLP-2019, pages 32–38,
Varna, Bulgaria, Sep 2–4, 2019.
https://doi.org/10.26615/issn.2603-2821.2019_006

narratives and medicine instruction leaflets are annotated and later aligned with the commonly used for this type of investigation tool GIZA++ (Och and Ney, 2003).

In following work, (Grishina and Stede, 2017) expand their approach with a new method. They present an annotation projection from multiple sources again with a trilingual parallel corpus of English, German and Russian. In both their articles, the authors use an annotation scheme similar to the guidelines of OntoNotes as it is the case in the work presented - an adapted version that holds also for Bulgarian is used.

Another corpus-based approach is employed by (Novak, 2018) with about 100 times bigger data compared to the previously mentioned works from the Prague Czech-English Dependency Treebank 2.0 (Nedoluzhko et al., 2016). Here, the word alignment is done again with GIZA++ and the analysis of the mention types is inspired by (Grishina and Stede, 2017) and even expanded with a new category, anaphoric zeros, which is essential for a pro-drop language like Czech.

In their next project, (Nedoluzhko et al., 2018) further investigate the cross-lingual coreference with the PAWS parallel treebank with texts in four languages - English, Czech, Russian and Polish - by annotating and analysing not only noun, but also verb phrases.

A different approach is presented by (Lapshinova-Koltunski et al., 2019) who use an English-German parallel corpus annotated manually with coreference information (ParCorFull) in order to discover, analyse and introduce a typology of differences in the coreference chains (referred to as 'incongruences').

Another line of research has its focus on the type of pronouns of the referential entities (Novak and Nedoluzhko, 2015). The authors thoroughly investigate the nature of the correspondences between the Polish and English chains by manually annotated alignments of coreferential expressions. Since the aim of the current research is to offer a preliminary outline of some specifics of coreference annotation in parallel English-Bulgarian texts, the model of analysis used in (Lapshinova-Koltunski et al., 2019) and the one of (Novak and Nedoluzhko, 2015) is applied in combination. The result is a typology of differences between Bulgarian and English coreference chains.

3 Annotation

As (Lapshinova-Koltunski et al., 2019) defines, no matter what pairs of languages are exemplified in the parallel texts for coreference annotation, there will always be some language-typology and translation-process-driven differences in the coreference chains. Besides the type of language and the type of translation (machine- or human-translated), the genre of the text has considerable impact as well. In the present research a piece of fictional literature is used, similarly to the approach of (Postolache et al., 2006).

Lots of parallel corpora used for cross-lingual coreference resolution consist of news articles (Nedoluzhko et al., 2018), (Novak, 2018) and some of them contain more than one type of texts (Grishina and Stede, 2015), (Grishina and Stede, 2017) .

The preliminary hypotheses concerning the types of annotation differences are:

- a missing coreference chain in the source text;

- a missing coreference chain in the target text;

- an identical coreference chain in both texts, but with different types of referential expressions;

- an identical coreference chain in both texts, but with different number of referential expressions;

- mismatching annotators decisions;

- annotation errors.

Some of the most obvious differences between the original and the translated text are as follows: a) the size of the text: "The Adventure of the Speckled Band" in English contains 608 sentences while the Bulgarian version - 647, and b) the total number of referential entities: 2133 in the first text, and only 1089 in the second. The source text has 329 coreference chains while the target text – only 190.

The texts were manually annotated with coreferences by two annotators working at first independently from each other and later - together with the web-based annotation tool WebAnno 2.3.1. (Yimam et al., 2014). The consequent analysis was done with the XML-based software system

CLaRK[2] (Simov et al., 2004). The additional processing with CLaRK was necessary because it works well with large texts and has no issues with languages and different encodings, which is not the case with WebAnno.

The annotation was done in accordance with the OntoNotes guidelines; at the same time some necessary modifications were made. Noun, adjective, adverb and pronoun antecedents and anaphora were annotated. The extension with event coreference and bridging anaphora is considered as one of the directions for future work. The modifications of the annotation scheme affect:

- subordinate clauses - in the OntoNotes guidelines these cases are taken for markables only if they contain the relative pronouns *which* and *who*, but in the current annotation, constructions with *when*, *where* and *that* are treated in the same way as the previous two;

- constructions of the type *only + plural noun* are considered generic;

- in constructions of the type *each of + noun/pronoun* only the noun or pronoun from the phrase are marked as referential expressions.

4 Typology of Differences

Annotation differences could be analysed and classified from various points of view. One possible approach is that of (Lapshinova-Koltunski et al., 2019), inspired by the work of (Klaudy and Karoly, 2005) on explicitation and implicitation in translation. (Lapshinova-Koltunski et al., 2019) present a typology of incongruences, outlining four types:

1. explicitation - it takes place when the translation contains more specific or new (not present in the source text) linguistic units; phrases are extended and sentences are split into two sentences;

2. implicitation - the translation is shorter than the source;

3. different interpretations - this is the case when annotators interpret the parallel texts in a different way;

4. annotation error - this concerns errors done during the manual annotation of the texts.

As considered by (Klaudy and Karoly, 2005), explicitations and implicitations may be:

- *obligatory* - their presence is motivated by the characteristics of the language and they serve to make the translation more comprehensible;

- *optional* - (Klaudy and Karoly, 2005) point out that in this case translators decide whether to apply explicitation or implicitation based on differences in language use, discourse structure, and background information.

The classification of (Novak and Nedoluzhko, 2015) distinguishes between three types:

1. central pronouns - this class includes personal, possessive, reflexive and reflexive possessive pronouns; the study shows that more than the half of all personal English pronouns turn out to be Czech anaphoric zeros.

2. relative pronouns - here pronominal adverbs are also added;

3. anaphoric zeros.

In our study the latter approach is applied, but also a deeper analysis of the nature of the annotation differences and examples is presented. It was stated earlier that the source text has almost 50 percent more coreference chains and referential entities than the target text. Most likely this substantial difference in quantity is due to the typical for Bulgarian zero anaphora. A lot of research has been devoted to that phenomenon, and it still seems to be the most sophisticated variety of anaphora, as noted by (Mitkov, 2002). For that reason, ellipsis is considered a separate class in the typology of annotation differences.

Zero Anaphora

This type of difference in the cross-lingual coreference annotation is very common. Probably every translator's basic aim is to give the translated text the most natural form possible, so the annotated Bulgarian version of "The Adventure of the Speckled Band" has lots of ellipses, especially zero pronominal anaphora:

---

[2]http://bultreebank.org/en/clark/

(1) Както виждам , пристигнали сте
     As   see-I , arrive-Part   were-you
     с   утринния влак .
     with morning-the train .
     'You have come in by train this morning, I
     see.'

The frequent omission of personal pronouns in
the text illustrated in (1) results in shorter coreference chains (with less referential entities) in the
translated story compared to the original. In the
next example, two phenomena can be observed: a
pronominal zero anaphora and an implicitation.

(2) Не издържам повече , ще полудея .
     No stand-I   no longer , shall go-I mad .
     'Sir, I can stand this strain no longer; I
     shall go mad if it continues.'

Because of the dropped personal pronoun, the
omission of the title *sir* and the phrase *this strain*,
there are no referential entities in the first clause
and the second clause has a short coreference
chain (*the strain, it*) with no analogue chain in the
target text.

An example for a zero noun anaphora with
cases as an antecedent is found in the following
sentence:

(3) Сред всичките тези случаи един от
     Among all-the these cases one of
     най-интересните безспорно е с
     most-interesting-the undoubtedly is with
     известния род [...] .
     famous-the family [...] .
     'Of all these varied cases, however, I can-
     not recall any which presented more sin-
     gular features [...] .'

All the types of zero anaphora defined in
(Mitkov, 2002) - pronominal, noun, verb, verb
phrase anaphora - are present in the target text,
however the ones including verbs are not in the
focus of this survey.

Explicitation and Implicitation

Numerous cases of explicitation and implicitation were observed in the Bulgarian translation of
A.C. Doyle's story. Most of them seem to be optional. This could be explained with the translator's decision, not necessarily with the specifics of
the language, as the following example illustrates:

(4) Настъпи дълго мълчание . Холмс
     (Followed a-long silence   . Holmes
     седеше   вторачен в огъня .
     was-sitting staring   in fire-the.)

'There was a long silence, during which
Holmes leaned his chin upon his hands
and stared upon the crackling fire.'

The "details" that the translator skipped (*his chin,
his hands*) would actually be parts of the coreferential chain if present in the Bulgarian sentence.

Other cases of explicitation might be observed
in examples like the next one where an English
sentence with a subordinate clause is divided into
two shorter sentences with the subordinate clause
transformed to main clause in Bulgarian:

(5) Жената   , в черни дрехи и с
     Woman-the , in black clothes and with
     плътен воал , седеше   до
     thick   veil , was-sitting-she by
     прозореца . Когато ни видя   ,
     window-the . When us saw-she ,
     веднага   стана   .
     immediately rose-she .
     'A lady dressed in black and heavily
     veiled, who had been sitting by the win-
     dow, rose as we entered.'

The Bulgarian version has a new markable, *the
veil*, which does not have an analogue in the English one.

The translation could rather easily lower the
number of markables with the means of explicitation:

(6) А   когато една млада жена се
     And when   one young woman se.Refl
     втурне толкова рано сутринта   през
     rushes so   early morning-the through
     столицата да буди   спящите   , със
     capital-the to wake up sleeping-the , with
     сигурност има да съобщи   нещо
     certainty   has to announce something
     много важно   .
     very   important .
     'Now, when young ladies wander about
     the metropolis at this hour of the morn-
     ing and knock sleepy people up out of
     their beds, I presume that it is something
     very pressing which they have to commu-
     nicate.'

In this example the markables *young
ladies/they, sleepy people/their* do not have
any correspondences in the target text.

Most Frequent Markables

Next sentences hint to one possible explanation
about why (and how) the target text ends up with
lower number of coreference chains and different
markables than the source text:

Pronoun type	Bulgarian	Mentions	English	Mentions
Personal	аз	18	I	224
Personal	ти	8	you	99
Personal	той	41	he	108
Personal	тя	22	she	56
Personal	ние	5	we	70

Table 1: Most frequent pronouns in the coreference chains.

(7) Майка ни умря скоро след нашето
Mother our died-she shortly after our
завръщане в Англия . Загина   преди
return   to England . Perish-she before
осем години при железопътна
eight years in   railway
катастрофа недалеч от   Кру .
accident   not far   from Crewe .

'Shortly after our return to England my
mother died — she was killed eight years
ago in a railway accident near Crewe.'

Here the combination of explicitation and zero
anaphora lead to the presence of new markables
and chains:

- *our (mother)* - (refers to *Helen and Julia*) will
  not have correspondence with the English *my
  (mother)* - referring only to *Helen*;

- *our (return)* - (refers to *Helen, Julia, their
  mother* and *their father*) will not have analogue in the Bulgarian text;

- *the mother* is literally mentioned once in
  the target text, because of the zero pronoun
  anaphora, and in the source text there are two
  expressions referring to her - *my mother, she.*

The following example illustrates a case of implicitation, in particular - a simplification of a
phrase:

(8) Тя спусна плътния си черен воал и
She dropped thick-the her black veil and
излезе .
left-she .

'She dropped her black thick veil over her
face and glided for the room .'

It cannot be concluded that the implicitation in
this case is obligatory - if the translation was literal
it would not make the sentence incomprehensible
or lead to unnecessary repetitions. The translator's
approach leads to the lack of two markables in the
target text - *her face and* the room.

The opposite process is also frequently observed:

(9) Усмивката се   разля още
Smile-the se-Refl. spread more
по-широко върху лицето на Холмс .
wider   on   face-the of Holmes .

'His smile broadened .'

With the optional explicitation the Bulgarian
sentence has three additional markables - *smile,
face* and *Holmes* unlike the English sentence with
two.

The observations with respect to the grammatical category of the annotated referential expressions in the Bulgarian text show that some of
the most frequent markables are proper nouns -
mainly names of the characters in the story, but
also names of locations. The total number of
proper nouns for main characters (which form the
longest coreference chains) is 135, of which, pre-
dictably, 68 are referring to Sherlock Holmes. In
the English version the results are similar - 122
proper nouns for character's names and 62 of them
referring to Holmes.

Other frequent markable from the class of personal pronouns is *he* (той) with 41 uses in Bulgarian and 108 in English, followed by the plural personal pronoun *you* (ви) with 123 mentions in the
source text and 26 in the target one. Another English possessive pronoun, *his*, has the remarkably
high frequency of 95 mentions. In the translation,
it is expressed by the Bulgarian reflexive possessive particle си (15 mentions) or with the short
form of the non-reflexive possessive form му (28
mentions).

As previously stated, subordinate English sentences are usually transformed and simplified in
the Bulgarian translation. The analysis of the
pronoun markables proves this observation once
again - there are 90 mentions of the relative pronoun *which*, and the other pronouns of this class
are also very common. However, the Bulgarian

corresponding forms are actually rare.

It can be concluded that zero pronoun anaphora are the main reason for the pronounced difference in terms of pronoun mentions frequency in the two languages. The results of the analysis of the central pronouns are very similar to the conclusions of (Novak and Nedoluzhko, 2015) based on the comparison between Czech and English coreference chains. The personal pronoun *I* has the highest rate of mentions in English while its Bulgarian analogue is rarely mentioned; the explanation for this phenomenon could be illustrated with examples of this kind:

(10) Познах гласа на сестра си
 Recognized-I voice-the of sister si.Refl
 [...] .

 'I knew that it was my sister's voice .'

5 Conclusions

The results from the observations made in the current study serve to support the creation of bigger quantities of coreference parallel corpora with Bulgarian as member of the language pair.

The existence of such corpora will allow for training a coreference resolver for Bulgarian and consequent experiments on the cross-lingual coreference resolution with Bulgarian.

This preliminary work might serve as a first draft for coreference annotation guidelines for Bulgarian, for the semi-automatic annotation of basic coreference chains, and with the creation of a larger bilingual corpus – for the fully automatic processing, as these are the directions of our future work. The next stage of the research is planned to include investigation of event coreference and bridging anaphora.

The work performed in this study is intended to serve as a base for a Ph.D. dissertation that would provide a thorough insight on the subject.

Acknowledgments

This work was partially supported by the Bulgarian Ministry of Education and Science under the National Research Programme "Young scientists and postdoctoral students" approved by DCM # 577 / 17.08.2018. Also the research reported here was partially funded by *the Bulgarian National Interdisciplinary Research e-Infrastructure for Resources and Technologies in favor of the Bulgarian Language and Cultural Heritage, part of the EU infrastructures CLARIN and DARIAH – CLaDA-BG*, Grant number DO01-164/28.08.2018.

References

Yulia Grishina and Manfred Stede. 2015. Knowledgelean projection of cireference chains across languages. In *Proceedings of the Eight Workshop on Building and Using Comparable Corpora*. Association for Coputational Linguistics.

Yulia Grishina and Manfred Stede. 2017. Multi-source annotation projection of coreference chains: Assessing strategies and testing opportunities. In *Proceedings of the 2nd Workshop on Coreference Resolution Beyond OntoNotes (CORBON 2017)*, Valencia, Spain. Association for Computational Linguistics.

Rebecca Hwa, Philip Resnik, Amy Weinberg, Clara Cabezas, and Okan Kolak. 2005. Bootstrapping parsers via syntactic projection across parallel texts. *Natural Language Engineering*.

Kinga Klaudy and Krisztina Karoly. 2005. Implicitation in translation: Empirical evidence for operational asymmetry in translation. *Across Languages and Cultures*.

Ekaterina Lapshinova-Koltunski, Sharid Loáiciga, Christian Hardmeier, and Pauline Krielke. 2019. Cross-lingual incongruences in the annotation of coreference. In *Proceedings of the Second Workshop on Computational Models of Reference, Anaphora and Coreference*. Association for Computational Linguistics.

Ruslan Mitkov. 2002. *Anaphora Resolution*. Longman, Great Britain.

Anna Nedoluzhko, Michal Novak, Silvie Cinkova, Marie Mikulova, and Jiri Mirovsky. 2016. Coreference in prague czech-english dependency treebank. In *Proceedings of the 10th International Conference on Language Resources and Evaluation (LREC 2016)*.

Anna Nedoluzhko, Michal Novak, and Maciej Ogrodniczuk. 2018. Paws: A multi-lingual parallel treebank with anaphoric relations. In *Proceedings of the First Workshop on Computational Models of Reference, Anaphora and Coreference*. Association for Computational Linguistics.

Michal Novak. 2018. A fine-grained large-scale analysis of coreference projection. In *Proceedings of the First Workshop on Computational Models of Reference, Anaphora and Coreference*. Association for Computational Linguistics.

Michal Novak and Anna Nedoluzhko. 2015. Correspondences between czech and english coreferential expressions. *Discours. Revue de linguistique, psycholinguistique et informatique*.

Franz Josef Och and Hermann Ney. 2003. A systematic comparison of various statistical alignment models. *Computational Linguistics*, 29(1):19–51.

Sebastian Pado and Mirella Lapata. 2005. Cross-linguistic projection of role-semantic information. In *Proceedings of Human Language Technology Conference and Conference on Empirical Methods in Natural Language Processing*, Vancouver, British Columbia, Canada. Association for Computational Linguistics.

Oana Postolache, Dan Cristea, and Constantin Orasan. 2006. Transferring coreference chains through word alignment. In *Proceedings of the Fifth International Conference on Language Resources and Evaluation*. European Language Resources Association.

Kiril Simov, Alexander Simov, Hristo Ganev, Krasimira Ivanova, and Ilko Grigorov. 2004. The CLaRK System: XML-based Corpora Development System for Rapid Prototyping. *Proceedings of LREC 2004*, pages 235–238.

David Yarowsky, Grace Ngai, and Richard Wicentowski. 2001. Inducing multilingual text analysis tools via robust projection across aligned corpora. In *Proceedings of the First International Conference on Human Language Technology Research*.

Seid Muhie Yimam, Richard Eckart de Castilho, Iryna Gurevych, and Chris Biemann. 2014. Automatic annotation suggestions and custom annotation layers in webanno. In *Proceedings of ACL-2014*. Association for Computational Linguistics.

Towards Accurate Text Verbalization for ASR Based on Audio Alignment

Diana Geneva and **Georgi Shopov**

IICT - BAS
2, Acad. G. Bonchev Str.
1113 Sofia, Bulgaria
{dageneva,gshopov}@lml.bas.bg

Abstract

Verbalization of non-lexical linguistic units plays an important role in language modeling for automatic speech recognition systems. Most verbalization methods require valuable resources such as ground truth, large training corpus and expert knowledge which are often unavailable. On the other hand a considerable amount of audio data along with its transcribed text are freely available on the Internet and could be utilized for the task of verbalization. This paper presents a methodology for accurate verbalization of audio transcriptions based on phone-level alignment between the transcriptions and their corresponding audio recordings. Comparing this approach to a more general rule-based verbalization method shows a significant improvement in ASR recognition of non-lexical units. In the process of evaluating this approach we also expose the indirect influence of verbalization accuracy on the quality of acoustic models trained on automatically derived speech corpora.

1 Introduction

Automatic speech recognition (ASR) systems transcribe utterances into sequences of linguistic units. Linguistic units can be roughly characterized as either lexical (e.g. "house", "seven", "second") or non-lexical – units that have different verbal and written form (e.g. "11", "02.07.2017", "cm"). The form of the linguistic units output from an ASR system depends on the units of the language model (LM). In order for an ASR system to be able to output certain linguistic units their phonetizations have to be known. This poses a problem because most LM training corpora contain both lexical and non-lexical units and while the phonetizations of most of the lexical units can be found in a pronunciation lexicon, this is not the case for the non-lexical units. Most of the methods addressing this issue follow one of two general approaches.

The first approach aims to verbalize the language model training corpus, i.e. to expand all non-lexical units to their verbal forms, and then train a verbal-domain language model on the resulting text that contains only lexical linguistic units (Chelba et al., 2010). Verbalization is often done using finite-state rewrite rules and is a non-trivial task since the choice of correct verbalization is ambiguous as it depends on the context in which the non-lexical unit is used. This approach has several disadvantages. Writing verbalization rules that make use of contextual information is a very time consuming task. It often requires domain specific knowledge and even then in many cases multiple correct verbalizations exist. On the other hand, context-independent rules select a single verbalization variant for each non-lexical unit which is usually very inaccurate because of the aforementioned ambiguities of written language. Alumäe et al. (2017) show how a small amount of verbalized text that serves as ground truth can be used to mitigate the lack of verbalization variability when using context-independent rules. Their method chooses a verbalization for each sentence by sampling from all of its possible verbalization variants with probability that is proportional to the probability of each individual variant. The probability of the variants is assigned by a language model trained on the ground truth text. Nevertheless, the verbalization may still be inaccurate due to the use of sampling.

The second approach is to train a written-domain language model on the original corpus that contains both lexical and non-lexical units and add

Proceedings of the Student Research Workshop associated with RANLP-2019, pages 39–47,
Varna, Bulgaria, Sep 2–4, 2019.
https://doi.org/10.26615/issn.2603-2821.2019_007

to the pronunciation lexicon the phonetizations of all non-lexical units from the language model vocabulary. Sak et al. (2013) show how this can be implemented without modifying the lexicon. They construct a verbalizer transducer that maps vocabulary items to verbal expansions and compose its inverse with the written-domain language model to produce a verbal-domain language model. This approach, however, is applicable mainly for very large training corpora where the size of the data alleviates the data sparsity issues caused by increasing the size of the language model vocabulary.

The increase of available multimedia content on the Internet and the development of speech and language technology in recent years have made it possible to significantly reduce the manual work needed to prepare speech and language resources. For example, the considerable amount of available audio data along with its transcribed text (such as audiobooks and recorded parliament plenary sessions) has been used for the creation of ASR corpora. The English ASR corpus LibriSpeech (Panayotov et al., 2015) has been derived from thousands of public domain audiobooks. Also, parliament session recordings have been utilized for building ASR corpora for Bulgarian (Geneva et al., in press), Catalan (Miró et al., 2014) and Icelandic (Helgadóttir et al., 2017).

In this paper we describe another way of taking advantage of such resources. We present a methodology for verbalization of audio transcriptions by decoding the corresponding audio with an ASR system and choosing the transcription verbalization that best matches the ASR output phonetically. The idea of using phonetic similarity is quite intuitive because it replicates what a human would do when faced with this task – to determine the correct verbal expansion of a non-lexical unit in a transcription he would have to frequently resort to listening to the audio. Using this methodology we aim to produce more accurate verbalization without the requirements of having large training corpora, ground truth or expert knowledge. Improvements in verbalization accuracy may lead not only to superior language models but could also indirectly improve the quality of acoustic models. Most of the ASR corpora derived from transcribed audio are based on automatic alignment of the audio with its transcription. For such tasks, having a more accurate verbalization method applied to the transcriptions would lead to better alignments and improved quality of the resulting speech corpus.

In the following sections we present the methodology for text verbalization described above and its application to the transcriptions of the plenary sessions of the Bulgarian Parliament. Section 2 describes the data available from the Bulgarian Parliament and the speech corpora and language resources we used to build an acoustic model for ASR. In Section 3 we apply a baseline verbalization method based on rewrite rules to the transcriptions of parliament speeches. In Section 4 we present the method of verbalization based on audio alignment and the process of applying it to the dataset from the Bulgarian Parliament described in Section 2. Finally, in Section 5 we measure the impact on ASR accuracy of the method described in Section 4 in comparison to the method from Section 3. We also provide evidence of the importance of verbalization accuracy to the quality of automatically derived speech corpora.

2 Data Preparation

2.1 Audio and Transcriptions

The website of the Bulgarian Parliament[1] provides video recordings of all plenary sessions since 2010 in mp4 format. The speeches are recorded using stationary directed microphones on the parliament's platform. The format of the audio stream in the video files is 44100 Hz mono compressed with the AAC codec at 75 kb/s. Each recording is separated into parts by the pause breaks made during the session. For each session the corresponding manually transcribed texts are provided in a single file. We downloaded the recordings and their transcriptions from 2010 until July 2018.

The preprocessing of the video files consisted of extracting the audio stream in 16 kHz PCM wav format using the ffmpeg[2] tool. The preparation of the transcriptions had to overcome several specific types of annotations that are present in the text but are not spoken in the audio. We will briefly discuss those issues. Geneva et al. (in press) treat them in more detail.

Every speech in the transcriptions is preceded by the name of the speaker and sometimes the name of his or her party written in free text.

---

[1] https://www.parliament.bg/
[2] https://ffmpeg.org

The text files also contain annotations that indicate what is happening in the room. All occurrences of both of those annotation types were consistently formatted and contained specific key-phrases which made it easy to construct regular expressions to remove them.

As mentioned above, for each session of the parliament there are several audio files but only one text transcription. We used the semi-automatic approach described by Geneva et al. (in press) to split the transcriptions so that they match the audio session parts. Despite of that, occasional inaccuracies still remain in the alignment of the session audio and text parts.

The resulting dataset consists of 1046 session recordings (2261 parts) for a total of 4832 hours of audio and 30 million words of text.

2.2 Acoustic Model

The Bulgarian ASR corpus BG-PARLAMA (Geneva et al., in press) is a speech corpus built from the speeches of the Bulgarian Parliament members. Its training set consists of 148607 speech segments from 572 unique speakers (422 male and 150 female) with a total duration of 249 hours.

We used the Kaldi ASR Toolkit (Povey et al., 2011) to train a time delay deep neural network (TDNN) (Peddinti et al., 2015) acoustic model with p-norm nonlinearities (Zhang et al., 2014) on the BG-PARLAMA corpus. A speaker-adaptive GMM model was also trained and used for generating state-level alignments for the TDNN training. We used the same parameters for the models as those in the LibriSpeech (Panayotov et al., 2015) Kaldi recipe. The phonetic system that we used is presented in (Mitankin et al., 2009; Hateva et al., 2016) and the pronunciation lexicon is the extended version (Geneva et al., in press) of the lexicon from (Mitankin et al., 2009).

3 Verbalization Based on Rules

In this section we describe the application of the verbalization method based on rewrite rules to the transcriptions from the Bulgarian Parliament. We use it as a baseline for comparison with the verbalization based on audio alignment described in Section 4.

3.1 Rules for Non-Lexical Units

In the transcriptions several frequently occurring types of non-lexical units are observed. They are presented in Table 1 alongside their frequencies and several example occurrences.

The verbalization of some of those units does not require contextual information and is therefore accomplished using simple rewrite dictionaries. The special symbols and some abbreviations fall under this category. Example lines from their rewrite dictionaries are shown below.

$$\S \longrightarrow \text{параграф}$$
$$\text{чл.} \longrightarrow \text{член}$$

There are also non-lexical units that require contextual information to uniquely determine their correct verbalization. In Table 1 only the metric units fall under this category. In general, the verbalization of a metric unit depends on the number preceding it. The singular form is used if the number is "1" and the plural otherwise. For example

$$\text{км.} \longrightarrow \text{километър}/1 \_$$
$$\text{км.} \longrightarrow \text{километра}/\text{Digit}^* - 1 \_$$

where $A \rightarrow B/L\_R$ denotes *"replace A with B when the left context is L and the right context is R"*.

The verbalization of the rest of the units from Table 1 (numbers, dates and times) is ambiguous because even though it requires contextual information, the correct verbalization is not uniquely determined by it. We will briefly discuss some of the causes for those ambiguities.

In Bulgarian numbers have cardinal and ordinal forms. Each form has three inflections based on gender (some of which coincide). Often more than one of these forms is a possible verbalization variant. For example, both the ordinal "алинея първа" and the cardinal "алинея едно" are correct verbalizations of "алинея 1". Another source of ambiguity is the fact that some numbers have doublet forms (e.g. "дванадесет" /dvanadeset/ and "дванайсет" /dvanayset/).

In colloquial speech it is common to omit whole parts of phrases. In date expressions the word for "year" is often left out as well as the words for "hours" and "minutes" in expressions for time. For years after 2000 the word for "thousands"("хиляди") is often skipped as in "две и втора" compared to "две хиляди и втора". For

Unit Type	Example Occurrences	Frequency
Arabic numbers	"21", "42"	865275
Roman numbers	"II", "XIV"	10200
Fractional numbers	"3.5", "25,03"	19488
Dates	"07.06.2019", "27 март 2019"	119209
Abbreviations	"чл.", "проф."	208216
Special symbols	"§", "№", "+"	105437
Metric units	"км.", "дка.", "лв."	87770
Times	"12 ч. и 23 мин.", "14,00 ч."	6229

Table 1: Most frequent non-lexical units found in the transcriptions.

years starting with "19" a shorter form is also accepted such as "деветдесет и четвърта"(ninety-fourth) for "1994".

In spite of the above-mentioned ambiguities, we verbalized numbers, dates and times using rewrite rules by choosing only one of the possible verbalization variants to expand all of their occurrences.

3.2 Recognition Errors

Before applying the verbalization rules described in the previous subsection the out-of-vocabulary words in the corpus were 4.97% using the extended lexicon from Section 2. After applying them we covered more than 99.65% of the vocabulary found in the transcriptions.

We trained a 3-gram modified Kneser-Ney smoothed language model on the verbalized text using the SRILM Toolkit (Stolcke, 2002). With this language model and the acoustic model described in Section 2 we decoded recordings of the Bulgarian Parliament from 2019 that contain relatively many non-lexical units. In the recognition results we observed systematic mistakes caused by the non-variability in the verbalization. The underlined words in the following snippet demonstrate some of the most common mistakes.

> ... за времето от шест до осемнай-
> сети юни ... гласували сто и едно
> народни представители ... създават
> се нова алинея две и алинея три ...
> десети октомври две хиляди и се-
> демнайсета година ...

The first underlined word is an example of incorrect usage of a cardinal instead of an ordinal number form. The second is a number form that should have agreed on gender with the word that follows it. Even though the cardinal number form

in the third and the fourth underlined words is permitted, it differs from the ordinal form that is spoken in the audio recording. The last underlined word should have been omitted because it is not pronounced at all.

We suspect that all those mistakes are caused by the language model. More specifically, because of the lack of variability in the verbalization of its training texts. The method presented in the next section corrects most of those mistakes and thus confirms our assumption.

4 Verbalization Based on Audio Alignment

In this section we present a method for verbalization of audio transcriptions based on phone-level alignment with the audio. Subsection 4.1 presents the creation of a written-domain language model from the transcribed texts and the extension of the pronunciation lexicon with all possible phonetizations of the non-lexical LM vocabulary items. Subsection 4.2 is devoted to the algorithm for phone-level alignment of the ASR output with the audio transcriptions. The algorithm is a modification of the classic algorithm for calculating the Levenshtein distance between strings. It allows to compute the Levenshtein distance between a given string and the concatenation of finite sets of strings. We prove the correctness of this algorithm in Appendix A.

4.1 Building Written-Domain LM and Extending the Lexicon

First, we identify the non-lexical words whose verbalization could not be uniquely determined. We tag them with special tags using rules based on those from the previous section. As seen in Table 1 the occurrences of time expressions are too few so they are treated alongside the unambiguous non-lexical words as described in Section 3.

We aim to add all possible phonetizations of those specially tagged units to the lexicon. However, this would lead to a major increase in the lexicon size. In order to avoid this we separate some of the tagged expressions into parts and add their phonetizations instead. For example instead of tagging whole date expressions such as "ᴛᴅ02.07.2017ᴛᴅ" we tag the day, month and year separately "ᴛᴅᴅ02ᴛᴅᴅ.ᴛᴅᴍ07ᴛᴅᴍ.ᴛᴅʏ2017ᴛᴅʏ". Non-integer numbers in decimal form are also separated into their integer and fractional parts. The different pronunciations of the decimal separator are also taken into consideration.

In order to reflect the specifics of the language more closely additional tags are introduced. Time periods are tagged separately from ordinary dates because "01–02 юни 2017" could be also pronounced with a "from-to" construction. In some cases a word could be omitted (such as the "year" word in date pronunciations) or a punctuation mark could be pronounced (e.g."dash" and "dot"). Thus new tags were introduced to reflect those specifics. Lastly, acronyms are also tagged separately because they have several pronunciation variants including their expanded form and several different letter-by-letter pronunciations.

The special tags, their frequencies and the verbalization variants that we deemed acceptable are presented in Table 2. We automatically generated the verbalization variants shown in the second column of Table 2 using rewrite rules compiled into finite-state transducers. The verbalizations were then processed using the phonetization rules from the Bulgarian Text-to-Speech System (Andreeva et al., 2005). The phonetization rules require accent information so the accent marks were manually added when needed. This resulted in the expansion of the lexicon with 31935 additional entries.

A 3-gram language model with modified Kneser-Ney smoothing was trained on the resulting tagged text and the updated lexicon. The Kaldi ASR Toolkit was used to decode the downloaded audio from the Bulgarian Parliament (see Section 2) using this language model and the acoustic model described in Section 2.

4.2 Phone-Level Alignment with Variants

The ASR system produces as output a sequence of words along with their recognized phonetiza-tions. Our aim is to align the specially tagged words in the transcribed text with this output in order to obtain their correct phonetizations (and therefore verbalizations). The simplest alignment scheme we could use is based on word-level Levenshtein distance. This technique is expected to align tagged units in the transcription with tagged units in the ASR output. In practice, however, very often an alternative written form is chosen by the ASR system. The reason for this is that the phonetization of a linguistic unit frequently coincides with a combination of the phonetizations of several other units. For example, the phonetization of "ᴛɴ101ᴛɴ" in the transcribed text is expected to be aligned to "ᴛɴ101ᴛɴ" in the ASR output. However, one of the phonetizations of "ᴛɴ101ᴛɴ" (/sto i edno/) coincides with phonetizations of "ᴛɴ100ᴛɴ и ᴛɴ1ᴛɴ" and "сто и едно". Because of this the ASR system could choose any of them and not specifically "ᴛɴ101ᴛɴ". This makes the word-level alignment inappropriate. Thus, we propose the use of phone-level alignment.

Looking at the ASR system output as a sequence of phones we aim to find its best alignment to any of the possible phonetizations of the transcribed text. Each phonetization is formed by the concatenation of possible phonetizations of its constituent words. If $w_1 w_2 ... w_n$ is the transcribed text and $\Phi(w_i)$ is the set of all possible phonetizations of w_i, then the resulting transcription phonetizations are $\Phi(w_1) \circ \Phi(w_2) \circ \cdots \circ \Phi(w_n)$ where $\circ$ denotes concatenation (see Appendix A). This could be used to solve the word-level alignment problem – in the example above, regardless of the word chosen by the ASR system, if the recognized phones are /sto i edno/, then the alignment will select the correct phonetization from $\Phi(\text{"ᴛɴ101ᴛɴ"})$. The corresponding verbalization could then be uniquely determined from the tagged unit and the chosen phonetization.

The algorithm (see Algorithm 1) is a modification of the Levenshtein distance algorithm (Wagner and Fischer, 1974) and takes into account all phonetization variants for each word in the transcribed text. Given a sequence of phones from the ASR system output $\alpha = a_1 a_2 \ldots a_n$, a sequence of words $\beta = b_1 b_2 \ldots b_m$ that represents a transcription text and a function Φ which yields all possible phonetizations of a given word, the algorithm finds the best alignment between all possible phonetizations of the transcribed text $\Phi(b_1) \circ$

Type	Verbalization Variants	Frequency
TN	doublet forms; ordinal; cardinal; all genders	808836
TRN	doublet forms; ordinal; cardinal; all genders	10194
TFN1	cardinal all genders	19488
TFN2	cardinal all genders; different decimal separator pronunciations	19488
TDD	doublet forms; ordinal masculine; optional leading zero	55765
TDM	doublet forms; ordinal masculine; optional leading zero; month name	2242
TDY	doublet forms; optional "thousands" word	104562
TDYW	optional	102136
TDDPERIOD	TDD variants and optional "from-to" construction	497
TDYPERIOD	TDY variants and optional "from-to" construction	4294
TPUNCT	optional	53298
TAC	expanded forms; different letter-by-letter pronunciations	67931

TN – arabic number, TRN – roman number, TFN1 – integer part of decimal non-integer, TFN2 – fractional part of decimal non-integer, TDD – day, TDM – month, TDY – year, TDYW – year word, TDDPERIOD – time period with dash between days, TDYPERIOD – time perid with dash between years, TPUNCT – some punctuation marks, TAC – abbreviations and acronyms

Table 2: Tagged non-lexical units.

$\Phi(b_2) \circ \cdots \circ \Phi(b_m)$ and α. For each $0 \leq i \leq n$ and $0 \leq j \leq m$ the best alignments between $\Phi(b_1) \circ \Phi(b_2) \circ \cdots \circ \Phi(b_i)$ and $a_1 a_2 \ldots a_j$ are stored in $\mathcal{M}[i][j]$. For each alignment in $\mathcal{M}[i-1]$ we choose the phonetization of b_i which best extends it and write it at the corresponding position in $\mathcal{M}[i]$. This is done in the for loop on line 8. LEVENSHTEINDISTANCE$(\varphi, \alpha, M[i-1])$ fills the dynamic programming table used for the computation of the Levenshtein distance between φ and α. It implements the standard Levenshtein algorithm described in (Wagner and Fischer, 1974). It uses $\mathcal{M}[i-1]$ as a first row, i.e. it extends the best alignments so far. The selection of the best extensions for each prefix of α is done in the for loop on line 10. In the end, $\mathcal{M}[m][n]$ contains the best alignment between $\Phi(b_1) \circ \Phi(b_2) \circ \cdots \circ \Phi(b_m)$ and α. The correctness of the algorithm is further discussed in Appendix A.

The proposed method is then applied to the transcribed texts. Since the agreement between the audio and its transcription is not perfect, we consider the different alignment situations between each tagged unit and the section in the ASR output it's aligned to. If a possible phonetization of the unit exactly matches its aligned section or is a substring of it, then this phonetization is chosen. Otherwise, we choose that phonetization of the unit which is within a given threshold distance (33% phone error rate in our case) to the aligned

section, if such exists. If none of those conditions are met, we choose a default phonetization based on the most frequent occurrences of the unit type. In Table 3 the frequency of those choices is shown.

Alignment Type	Frequency
Exact matches	919122
Substring matches	36132
Levenshtein distance $\leq 33\%$	95960
Remaining (default)	197517

Table 3: Frequency of phonetization choices based on the phone-level alignment.

5 Results

During the preliminary tests with the verbalization method from Section 4 we observed that many of the recognition errors described in Section 3 were still present. For example, even though both "алинея едно" and "алинея първа" occur in the language model from Section 4, the ordinal form "алинея първа" was consistently recognized as the cardinal "алинея едно". This lead us to believe that the problem lies within the acoustic model. The texts of the BG-PARLAMA training set contain only occurrences of the cardinal form. We supposed that non-variability in the verbalization used for the preparation of BG-PARLAMA

44

Algorithm 1 Pseudocode of the phone-level alignment algorithm with variants.

1: $\mathcal{F} \leftarrow$ phones in the phonetization system
2: $\mathcal{D} \leftarrow$ language model vocabulary
3: $\Phi \leftarrow$ function that maps every word in $\mathcal{D}$ to a finite set of its phonetizations
4: $\alpha \leftarrow$ sequence of phones $a_1 a_2 \ldots a_n \in \mathcal{F}^*$ output from an ASR system
5: $\beta \leftarrow$ sequence of words $b_1 b_2 \ldots b_m \in \mathcal{D}^*$ that represents a transcription text
6: $\mathcal{M} \leftarrow$ an $(m+1) \times (n+1)$ matrix such that $\mathcal{M}[0][j] = j$ for $0 \le j \le n$ and $\mathcal{M}[i][j] = \infty$ for $1 \le i \le m$ and $0 \le j \le n$
7: **for** $i \leftarrow 1, m$ **do**
8:     **for all** $\varphi \in \Phi(b_i)$ **do**
9:         $\mathcal{M}' \leftarrow \textsc{LevenshteinDistance}(\varphi, \alpha, \mathcal{M}[i-1])$
10:         **for** $j \leftarrow 0, n$ **do**
11:             $\mathcal{M}[i][j] \leftarrow \textsc{Min}(\mathcal{M}[i][j], \mathcal{M}'[|\varphi|][j])$
12:         **end for**
13:     **end for**
14: **end for**
---

lead to mismatches between the audio and its text. In order to test this hypothesis we removed all speeches from the corpus which contain the word "едно" and trained a new TDNN acoustic model with the same parameters. Using this acoustic model and the language model from Section 4 the above-mentioned mistakes were corrected which confirmed the hypothesis. Similar recognition errors caused by the speech corpus were observed between doublet forms of numbers.

Since the number of non-lexical units in the transcriptions is significantly lower than the number of lexical units, we use a similar metric to that in (Sak et al., 2013). Instead of word error rate (WER) we compute non-lexical unit error rate (NER) defined as:

$$\frac{ND + NI + NS}{NN}$$

where NN is the total number of non-lexical number and ND, NI and NS are respectively the number of deletions, insertions and substitutions of non-lexical units. We compared the NER of two ASR systems based on the acoustic model described above that differ only in the language model – the first uses the LM from Section 3, while the second uses the LM from Section 4. The test and dev sets of BG-PARLAMA contain hardly any non-lexical units. This is why the ASR systems were used to decode the specially chosen parliament session from the 5th of June 2019. It contains 758 non-lexical units which we manually transcribed. Examination of the recognition results revealed that many of the mistakes

were caused by the system choosing the wrong number doublet form. As we already mentioned, those mistakes are the result of imperfections in the speech corpus. Thus, they should not be included in the verbalization performance comparison. The NER with the first and second LM are shown in Table 4. As it can be seen, the verbalization method presented in Section 4 halved the NER of the verbalization method described in Section 3. Investigation of the recognition errors proved that the alignment-based method is able to correct many of the errors caused by the non-variability of the rule-based method. In order to achieve better estimate of the improvement the aforementioned mismatches present in the speech corpus would have to be reduced.

Verbalization Method	NER
Based on rules	22.8%
Based on alignment	11.5%

Table 4: Non-lexical error rate on the parliament session from the 5th of July 2019.

6 Conclusion

In this paper we described a method for text verbalization based on phone-level alignment between transcriptions and their corresponding audio recordings. We compared it to a general rule-based verbalization method and showed significant reduction in the recognition error rate of non-lexical units. The comparison tests showed that verbalization plays an important role not only in language modeling but it could indirectly affect the quality of acoustic models as well. We plan to further analyze the mistakes we discovered in the BG-PARLAMA corpus and explore how more accurate verbalization methods could lead to better automatically derived speech corpora.

Acknowledgments

The research presented in this paper is partially funded by the Bulgarian Ministry of Education and Science via National Science Program "Electronic healthcare in Bulgaria" (e-Zdrave) grant DO1-200/2018 and National Science Program "Information and Communication Technologies for Unified Digital Market in Science, Education and Security" grant DO1-205/2018.

References

Tanel Alumäe, Andrus Paats, Ivo Fridolin, and Einar Meister. 2017. Implementation of a Radiology Speech Recognition System for Estonian Using Open Source Software. In *INTERSPEECH*.

Maria Andreeva, Ivaylo Marinov, and Stoyan Mihov. 2005. SpeechLab 2.0: A High-Quality Text-to-Speech System for Bulgarian. In *Proceedings of the RANLP International Conference 2005*. pages 52–58.

Ciprian Chelba, Johan Schalkwyk, Thorsten Brants, Vida Ha, Boulos Harb, Will Neveitt, Carolina Parada, and P. S. Xu. 2010. Query language modeling for voice search. *2010 IEEE Spoken Language Technology Workshop* pages 127–132.

Diana Geneva, Georgi Shopov, and Stoyan Mihov. in press. Building an ASR Corpus Based on Bulgarian Parliament Speeches. In *Proceedings of the SLSP*.

Neli Hateva, Petar Mitankin, and Stoyan Mihov. 2016. BulPhonC: Bulgarian Speech Corpus for the Development of ASR Technology. In *Proceedings of the Tenth International Conference on Language Resources and Evaluation LREC 2016, Portorož, Slovenia, May 23-28, 2016*. pages 771–774. http://www.lrec-conf.org/proceedings/lrec2016/summaries/478.html.

Inga Rún Helgadóttir, Róbert Kjaran, Anna Björk Nikulásdóttir, and Jón Guonason. 2017. Building an ASR Corpus Using Althingi's Parliamentary Speeches. In *Proc. INTERSPEECH*. pages 2163–2167. https://doi.org/10.21437/Interspeech.2017-903.

Xavier Anguera Miró, Jordi Luque, and Ciro Gracia. 2014. Audio-to-text alignment for speech recognition with very limited resources. In *INTERSPEECH*. pages 1405–1409.

Petar Mitankin, Stoyan Mihov, and Tinko Tinchev. 2009. Large vocabulary continuous speech recognition for Bulgarian. In *Proceedings of the RANLP 2009*. pages 246–250.

V. Panayotov, G. Chen, D. Povey, and S. Khudanpur. 2015. Librispeech: An ASR corpus based on public domain audio books. In *2015 IEEE International Conference on Acoustics, Speech and Signal Processing (ICASSP)*. pages 5206–5210. https://doi.org/10.1109/ICASSP.2015.7178964.

Vijayaditya Peddinti, Daniel Povey, and Sanjeev Khudanpur. 2015. A time delay neural network architecture for efficient modeling of long temporal contexts. In *INTERSPEECH*.

Daniel Povey, Arnab Ghoshal, Gilles Boulianne, Lukas Burget, Ondrej Glembek, Nagendra Goel, Mirko Hannemann, Petr Motlicek, Yanmin Qian, Petr Schwarz, Jan Silovsky, Georg Stemmer, and Karel Vesely. 2011. The Kaldi Speech Recognition Toolkit. In *IEEE 2011 Workshop on Automatic Speech Recognition and Understanding*. IEEE Signal Processing Society. IEEE Catalog No.: CFP11SRW-USB.

Hasim Sak, Françoise Beaufays, Kaisuke Nakajima, and Cyril Allauzen. 2013. Language model verbalization for automatic speech recognition. *2013 IEEE International Conference on Acoustics, Speech and Signal Processing* pages 8262–8266.

Andreas Stolcke. 2002. SRILM - an extensible language modeling toolkit. In *INTERSPEECH*.

Robert A. Wagner and Michael J. Fischer. 1974. The String-to-String Correction Problem. *J. ACM* 21(1):168–173. https://doi.org/10.1145/321796.321811.

X. Zhang, J. Trmal, D. Povey, and S. Khudanpur. 2014. Improving deep neural network acoustic models using generalized maxout networks. In *2014 IEEE International Conference on Acoustics, Speech and Signal Processing (ICASSP)*. pages 215–219. https://doi.org/10.1109/ICASSP.2014.6853589.

A Correctness of the Alignment with Variants

We will make use of some standard terms from formal language theory. We call an alphabet any finite set of symbols. A string over some alphabet is a finite sequence of symbols from that alphabet. With $|\alpha|$ we denote the length of a string α, i.e. the length of the corresponding sequence. We will use ε to denote the unique string of length 0 and Σ^* to denote the set of all strings over the alphabet Σ. The operation "concatenation of strings" and its lifted version to sets of strings will be denoted with $\circ$. That is for the strings $\alpha = a_1 a_2 \dots a_n$ and

$\beta = b_1 b_2 \ldots b_m, \alpha \circ \beta = a_1 a_2 \ldots a_n b_1 b_2 \ldots b_m$ and for the sets of strings A and B, $A \circ B = \{\alpha \circ \beta \mid \alpha \in A \wedge \beta \in B\}$.

The Levenshtein distance between two strings s_1 and s_2 is defined as the minimum number of operations (insertions, deletions and substitutions) that transform s_1 into s_2. This can be formalized as follows.

Definition 1. Let Σ be an alphabet. We define the set

$$op(\Sigma) := \{(a, b) \mid a, b \in \Sigma \cup \{\varepsilon\} \wedge (a, b) \neq (\varepsilon, \varepsilon)\},$$

and the function $w \colon op(\Sigma) \rightarrow \{0, 1\}$ as $w((a, b)) = 0$ iff $a = b$, for any $(a, b) \in op(\Sigma)$.

Definition 2. Let Σ be an alphabet and $\alpha, \beta \in \Sigma^*$. An *alignment* of α and β is a string $\gamma \in op(\Sigma)^*, \gamma = (a_1, b_1)(a_2, b_2) \ldots (a_n, b_n)$ such that $\alpha = a_1 \circ a_2 \circ \ldots \circ a_n$ and $\beta = b_1 \circ b_2 \circ \ldots \circ b_n$. The *weight* of γ is $\widehat{w}(\gamma) = \sum_{i=1}^{n} w((a_i, b_i))$. We use $ali(\alpha, \beta)$ to denote the set of all alignments of α and β.

Definition 3. The Levenshtein distance between the strings $\alpha \in \Sigma^*$ and $\beta \in \Sigma^*$ is defined as

$$lev(\alpha, \beta) := \min\{\widehat{w}(\gamma) \mid \gamma \in ali(\alpha, \beta)\}.$$

Definition 4. The Levenshtein distance between a string $\alpha \in \Sigma^*$ and a set of strings $B \subseteq \Sigma^*$ is defined as

$$\widehat{lev}(\alpha, B) := \min \bigcup_{\beta \in B} \{\widehat{w}(\gamma) \mid \gamma \in ali(\alpha, \beta)\}.$$

In our case we have an alphabet $\mathcal{F}$ – the phones in the phonetization system, an alphabet $\mathcal{D}$ – the words in the LM vocabulary, and a function $\Phi \colon \mathcal{D} \to \mathcal{P}(\mathcal{F}^*)$ which maps every word in $\mathcal{D}$ to a finite set (the phonetizations of the word). Given the phone output of the ASR system $\alpha \in \mathcal{F}^*, \alpha = a_1 a_2 \ldots a_n$, and $\beta \in \mathcal{D}^*$, $\beta = b_1 b_2 \ldots b_m$ – the words in the transcription text, we look for the Levenshtein distance between α and the set $\Phi(b_1) \circ \Phi(b_2) \circ \ldots \circ \Phi(b_m)$. We will use α_i and β_i to denote the prefixes of respectively α and β of length i. We will also write $\Phi(\beta_i)$ instead of $\Phi(b_1) \circ \ldots \circ \Phi(b_i)$. As already mentioned, the LEVENSHTEINDISTANCE function from Algorithm 1 implements the standard Levenshtein algorithm using a predefined first row for the dynamic programming table. Its correctness follows directly from the correctness of the Levenshtein algorithm and is expressed in Proposition 1.

Proposition 1. *Let* $\varphi \in \Phi(b_{i+1})$. *If* $\mathcal{M}' = $ LEVENSHTEINDISTANCE(φ, α, X) *where* $X[j] = \widehat{lev}(\alpha_j, \Phi(\beta_i))$ *for* $0 \leq j \leq n$, *then* $\mathcal{M}'[|\varphi|][j] = \widehat{lev}(\alpha_j, \Phi(\beta_i) \circ \{\varphi\})$.

Proof. Straightforward induction on $|\varphi|$. $\square$

In order to demonstrate the correctness of Algorithm 1, i.e. to show that $\mathcal{M}[m][n]$ is the Levenshtein distance between α and $\Phi(\beta_m)$, it is enough to prove the following proposition.

Proposition 2. *For every* $0 \leq i \leq m$ *at the end of the* $i - th$ *iteration of the for loop beginning on line 7*

$$(\forall 0 \leq j \leq n)(\mathcal{M}[i][j] = \widehat{lev}(\alpha_j, \Phi(\beta_i)),$$

where for $i = 0$ *we assume that* $\Phi(\beta_i) = \{\varepsilon\}$.

Proof. We will prove it by induction on i.

For $i = 0$ the proposition becomes

$$(\forall 0 \leq j \leq n)(\mathcal{M}[0][j] = \widehat{lev}(a_1 a_2 \ldots a_j, \{\varepsilon\})$$
$$= lev(a_1 a_2 \ldots a_j, \varepsilon)).$$

Since $\mathcal{M}[0][j] = j$ for $0 \leq j \leq n$ as defined on line 6 and $lev(a_1 a_2 \ldots a_j, \varepsilon) = j$ by definition, the base case holds. Let the proposition hold for some $0 \leq i \leq m - 1$. Let $\varphi \in \Phi(b_{i+1})$. Proposition 1 implies that $\mathcal{M}'[|\varphi|][j] = \widehat{lev}(\alpha_j, \Phi(\beta_i) \circ \{\varphi\})$. The for loop on line 10 takes the minimum for each j. Therefore

$$\mathcal{M}[i + 1][j] = \min_{\varphi \in \Phi(b_{i+1})} \mathcal{M}'[|\varphi|][j]$$
$$= \min_{\varphi \in \Phi(\beta_{i+1})} \widehat{lev}(\alpha_j, \Phi(\beta_i) \circ \{\varphi\})$$
$$= \min_{\varphi \in \Phi(\beta_{i+1})} \bigcup_{\lambda \in \Phi(\beta_i) \circ \{\varphi\}} \{\widehat{w}(\gamma) \mid \gamma \in ali(\alpha_j, \lambda)\}$$
$$= \min \bigcup_{\lambda \in \Phi(\beta_{i+1})} \{\widehat{w}(\gamma) \mid \gamma \in ali(\alpha_j, \lambda)\}$$
$$\stackrel{\text{def}}{=} \widehat{lev}(\alpha_j, \Phi(\beta_{i+1})). \qquad \square$$

Evaluation of Stacked Embeddings for Bulgarian on the Downstream Tasks
POS and NERC

Iva Marinova
LMaKP
IICT-BAS
Sofia, Bulgaria
iva.marinova@identrics.net

Abstract

This paper reports on experiments with different stacks of word embeddings and evaluation of their usefulness for Bulgarian downstream tasks such as Named Entity Recognition and Classification (NERC) and Part-of-speech (POS) Tagging. Word embeddings stay in the core of the development of NLP, with several key language models being created over the last two years like FastText (Bojanowski et al., 2017), ElMo (Peters et al., 2018), BERT (Devlin et al., 2018) and Flair (Akbik et al., 2018). Stacking or combining different word embeddings is another technique used in this paper and still not reported for Bulgarian NERC. Well-established architecture is used for the sequence tagging task such as BI-LSTM-CRF, and different pre-trained language models are combined in the embedding layer to decide which combination of them scores better.

1 Introduction

In this paper are reported the initial experiments for my PhD project which final goal is to build a system for extraction and classification of named entities, events and the relations between them from Bulgarian texts. The evaluation of the recent language models for Bulgarian is sufficient for my future work as it involves tasks such as NERC, Event Classification and Relation Extraction. All of them are considered downstream tasks and are often used to evaluate the language models and their usefulness. Currently, the tasks Event Classification and Relation Extraction are not addressed sufficiently. The data is available within the Bulgarian National Research Infrastructure for Language, Culture and History Resources and Tools — CLaDA-BG. In further experiments I will proceed with these data.

NERC and Event classification are considered both as sequence tagging tasks. Such tasks in the available manually annotated data from BulTreeBank (BTB) Project (Simov et al., 2002) are the part-of-speech tags and the named entities encoded in IOB (inside-outside-beginning) format.

Recent work on sequence tagging shows that BI-LSTM-CRF as proposed by (Huang et al., 2015) is the dominant solution applied to many different languages. This paper introduced the BIdirectional LSTM with CRF classfier (denoted as BI-LSTM-CRF) model to NLP sequence tagging tasks. The authors show that their model can efficiently use both past and future input features due to the bidirectional application of the LSTM component and use the sentence level tag information thanks to the CRF layer. This architecture reports state-of-the-art accuracy on POS, chunking and NERC tasks.

Here NERC and POS tagging are employed as fundamental tasks for the future experiments with Named Entity Recognition, Event Classification and Relation Extraction for Bulgarian texts. The next step will be to simultaneously solve these tasks together in a combined multitask model. These experiments should improve the interaction with linguistic information for Bulgarian.

The structure of the paper is as follows: the next section outlines the related work; description of the architecture and results of the experiments are available in Section 3; the last section concludes the paper and provides some ideas for future work.

2 Related Work

The identification of named entity (NE) mentions in texts is often implemented using a sequence tag-

Proceedings of the Student Research Workshop associated with RANLP-2019, pages 48–54,
Varna, Bulgaria, Sep 2–4, 2019.
https://doi.org/10.26615/issn.2603-2821.2019_008

ger, where each token is labeled with an IOB tag, indicating whether the token is beginning of a NE — (B), whether it is inside of a NE (I) or it is outside of a NE (O). This type of annotation is first proposed at CoNLL-2003 (Tjong Kim Sang and De Meulder, 2003). The Bulgarian data is annotated with the same tags as the proposed in the above publication: B-PER, I-PER, B-ORG, I-ORG, B-LOC, I-LOC, B-MISC, I-MISC, and O. In this way not only the structure of the NE is represented, but also its category. An example of an annotated sentence — Върна ли книгата на Петър Илиев? (Did you return the book to Peter Iliev?) — from the BulTreeBank is given here:

Върна	O
ли	O
книгата	O
на	O
Петър	B-PER
Илиев	I-PER
?	O

The NE *Peter Iliev* is annotated with the tags for PERSON marking the first token as a beginning of the NE and the second token as an internal token of the same NE. All other tokens are annotated by the tag O as outside tokens.

This dataset is used in some of the works on Bulgarian NERC, but in different splits and/or with some additions explained further.

(Georgiev et al., 2009) employ a rich set of features in their solution. At that time, CRFs was the dominant approach to NERC, but it required extensive and manual feature engineering, especially for morphological rich languages like Bulgarian. Their work was mostly devoted to construct a set of orthographic and domain-specific features. Using gazetteers, local/non-local morphology, feature induction and mutual information in the form of unlabeled texts they achieve **F1=89.40**. They used a development set during the training in order to improve the model and finally evaluated the model over the test set. The data split sizes are as follows: the training set contains 8,896 sentences; the development set contains 1,779 sentences; and the testing set contains 2,000 sentences.

The same data from BTB, with some additional data, is used by (Simeonova et al., 2019). The difference is that the supplement was annotated only on token level and the original data was annotated syntactically. In the current experiments this addition is not used.

(Simeonova et al., 2019) use LSTM-CRF on top of a word embedding layer too, but the authors employ morphosyntactic features in the data, using the position-aware morphosyntactic tags proposed by (Simov and Osenova, 2004). The word embeddings used in their experiments are Bulgarian FastText Vectors by (Bojanowski et al., 2017). They form the final vector representations of the word by combining FastText with character embeddings and further improve the test scores with POS and morphological representations. The best score achieved by their system is **F1=92.20**.

Since the data split used by (Georgiev et al., 2009) was not found and the new data used by (Simeonova et al., 2019) were not used in these experiments, the results from the experiments reported in this paper are not directly comparable with theirs.

Recently the Second Multilingual Named Entity Challenge in Slavic languages (Piskorski et al., 2019) explores the NERC task as part of a more complex solution including recognizing mentions of named entities in Web documents, their normalization, and cross-lingual linking. The challenge was performed on four languages including Bulgarian. The best achieved score for Bulgarian is **F1=87.5**. The data annotated within the shared task is in different format and is not used in my experiments.

There are many more works devoted to the POS tagging task for Bulgarian such as (Georgiev et al., 2012) and (Popov, 2016). (Georgiev et al., 2012) use guided learning, lexicon and rules and explore different tag sets achieving accuracy of 97.98, 98.85 and 99.30 with respectively 680, 49 and 13 tags.

Here their Table 5 is extended with results from the experiments done after the publishing of (Georgiev et al., 2012) including my own . Consult Table 1 for the complete overview. In the next section the experiment setup and the achieved results are described further.

3 Experiments

For the development of the models is used Flair[1], an NLP library implemented by Zalando Research on top of PyTorch[2]. Apart from their own pre-trained Flair contextualized string embeddings

---

[1] https://github.com/zalandoresearch/flair
[2] https://pytorch.org/

Tool/Authors	Method	Tags	Acc.
Tree Tagger	Decision Trees	680	89.2
ACOPOST	Memory-based learning	680	89.91
SVMTool	SVM	680	92.22
TnT	HMM	680	92.53
(Georgiev et al., 2009)	Guided learning	680	90.34
(Simov and Osenova, 2001)	RNN	160	92.87
(Georgiev et al., 2009)	Guided learning	95	94.4
(Savkov et al., 2011)	SVM + Lexicon + Rules	680	94.65
Tanev and Mitkov 2002	Rules	303	95.00
(Simov and Osenova, 2001)	RNN	15	95.17
Doychinova and Mihov 2004	Transform-based learning	40	95.50
Doychinova and Mihov 2004	Rules + Lexicon	40	98.40
(Georgiev et al., 2012)	Guided learning	680	95.72
(Georgiev et al., 2012)	Guided learning + Lexicon	680	**97.83**
(Georgiev et al., 2012)	Guided learning + Lexicon + Rules	680	97.98
(Georgiev et al., 2012)	Guided learning + Lexicon + Rules	49	98.85
(Georgiev et al., 2012)	Guided learning + Lexicon + Rules	**13**	**99.30**
(Popov, 2016)	BiLSTM Word Embeddings 100 (neurons)	153	91.45
(Popov, 2016)	BiLSTM Word Embeddings 125 (neurons)	153	91.13
(Popov, 2016)	BiLSTM Word + Suffix Embeddings 125 (neurons)	153	94.47
(Plank et al., 2016)	BiLSTM	16	97.97
(Yu et al., 2017)	CNN	16	98.23
(Yasunaga et al., 2017)	Adversarial training	16	98.53
experiment 1	BI-LSTM-CRF + Stacked embeddings (bg + flair-fast + char)	**16**	**98.90**
experiment 2	BI-LSTM-CRF + Stacked embeddings (bg + flair + char)	**16**	**99.10**

Table 1: Summary of all available POS systems for Bulgarian with different tag sets.

(Akbik et al., 2019b), the library provides access to many other state-of-the-art language models, such as FastText (Grave et al., 2018), Glove (Pennington et al., 2014), Elmo (Peters et al., 2018), BERT (Devlin et al., 2018).

Stacking the embeddings is one of the most important features of the library and the functionality is used in the experiments to concatenate language models together as the developers claim that this method often gives best results and lately has become a common technique in sequence labeling models.

3.1 NE Recognition and Classification

The BTB dataset consist of 14,732 sentences from different genres like newspapers articles, legal documents — the Bulgarian Constitution, some user generated data, literature, etc. Data is split into training, development, and test sets. The sizes of the sets are as follows: the training set contains 10,979 sentences; the development set contains 1,487 sentences; and the testing set contains 2,266 sentences.

The hyperparameters used to train the BI-LSTM-CRF are as follows: the hidden vector size is 256; the learning rate is set to 0.1; the sequence length is 250; mini batch size is 32; and number of max epochs is 150. The model architecture as

defined by (Huang et al., 2015) is depicted on Figure 1.

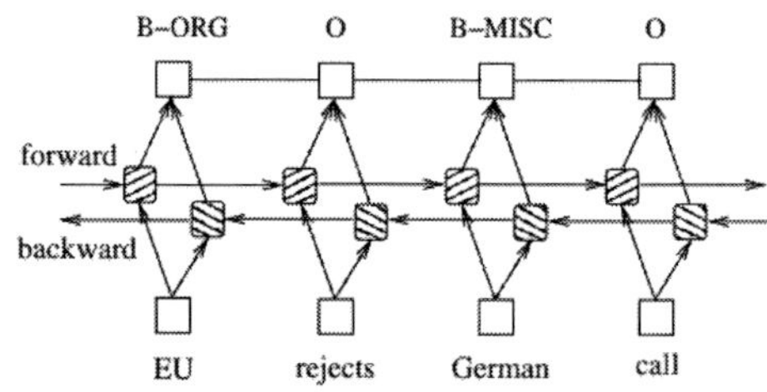

Figure 1: Bidirectional LSTM-CRF for Sequence Tagging (Huang et al., 2015)

The pre-trained language models used for the embedding layer are the following:

First, **BERT-base-multilingual-cased** model trained by (Devlin et al., 2018). This is their multilingual model. It is trained on 104 languages — the top languages with the largest Wikipedias. The model is implement as a 12-layer, 768-hidden, 12-heads, 110M parameters Bidirectional Transformer.

Second, **Bulgarian flair-forward and -backward** model trained by Stefan Schweter.[3] The author of the forward and backward Bulgarian

[3] https://github.com/stefan-it

language models uses data from recent Wikipedia dump and corpora from OPUS. Training was done for one epoch over the full training corpus, which in Bulgarian consists of 111,336,781 tokens.

The hyperparameters used to train the contextual string embeddings are the following: the hidden vector size is 2048; the number of the hidden layers is 1; the sequence length is 250; and the mini batch size is 100,

One model is trained in a forward direction and one backward and combining them by concatenation contributes to the contextual vector representation of the words. There are two available -forward and -backward coupled models for Bulgarian:

bg-forward,bg-backward

and

bg-forward-fast,bg-backward-fast

The -fast models are CPU friendly and lightweight to train allowing for easy experimentation with a little damage to the result. The authors use vanilla SGD with no momentum, clipping gradients at 5 and employ a simple learning rate annealing method in which they halve the learning rate if training loss does not fall for 5 consecutive epochs (Akbik et al., 2018). The contextualization of the words is given by the utilization of the hidden states of the forward-backward recurrent neural network. From this forward-backward language model, they concatenate both the output hidden state after the last character in the word using the forward language model and semantic-syntactic information from the end of the sentence to this character with the backward language model. Both output hidden vector states are concatenated to form the final embedding and capture the semantic-syntactic information of the word itself as well as its surrounding context.

Another language model used in the experiments is **FastText**[4] obtained using CBOW ((Mikolov et al., 2013)) with position-weights, in dimension 300, character n-grams of length 5, a window of size 5 and 10 negatives as described in Learning Word Vectors for 157 Languages by (Grave et al., 2018).

The other embeddings used in the experiments are Character and OneHot embeddings obtained from the corpus. The Flair authors describe the use of stacked embedding in (Akbik et al., 2019a).

Results for NERC task

Table 2 shows the results of the experiments on the NERC task where the abbreviations in the left column represent the language models used from the following list:

1. **bg** = FastText wiki embeddings

2. **flair-fast** = bg-forward-fast + bg-backward-fast

3. **flair** = bg-forward + bg-backward

4. **char** = Character Embeddings

5. **onehot** = OneHot Embeddings

6. **bert** = bert-base-multilingual-cased

Model	Micro F1
bg + char	96.18
bg + flair-fast	95.75
bg + flair + char	**96.29**
bg + flair + onehot	96.21
bg + bert + char	86.08
bert + flair	83.37

Table 2: Evaluation of stacked embeddings for Bulgarian NERC.

From Table 2 it can be concluded that the best performing stack of embeddings is the concatenation of FastText, bg-forward, bg-backward, and Character embeddings. Table 3 shows the best results for the combinations of embeddings the per class.

Class	P	R	F1
LOC	95.54	96.62	96.08
ORG	95.28	93.74	94.50
MISC	97.14	82.93	89.47
PER	97.68	98.56	98.12

Table 3: Per class results from the best model. Precision (P), Recall (R) and F1

The combination of word embeddings, character embeddings, and the contextual string embeddings outperforms the other combinations, because in this way the words in the text are vectorized with respect to their contextual meaning and they are further represented as a bag of character n-grams. A vector representation is associated to each character n-gram and thus words are represented as the sum of these representations. These models are fast and lightweight for training of the task. I am going to use them further in the experiments on the other tasks.

BERT (bert-base-multilingual-cased) did not improved the scores in these experiments, being most inaccurate in the classification of the MISC class, scoring particularly with Precision=64.71, Recall=40.24 and F1=49.62. Furthermore, the training of BI-LSTM-CRF with this language model is slow and needs a lot of computational resources.

Originally BERT (particularly bert-base-multilingual-cased) is tested on the XNLI dataset for machine translation on 6 out of 15 languages included in the data. The multilingual model scored 3% worse on English and Chinese than the single-language models for these languages. In my future work I envisage a training of a custom BERT embeddings for the Bulgarian in order to improve it's behaviour on the downstream tasks. Furthermore, the authors claim that the main idea behind BERT and the reason to propose it is to improve the fine-tuning based approaches, thus in the future experiments with Bulgarian NERC the idea should be tested. Fine-tuning is done by first initializing the language model with the pre-trained parameters, and all of the parameters are then fine-tuned using the labeled data from the custom corpus.

3.2 POS Tagging

The method used in the experiments with POS tagging is the same as the method used for NERC task presented above. POS tagging and NERC are both sequence tagging tasks so there is no need to change the proven architecture of the BI-LSTM-CRF tagger on top of the embedding layer. Moreover, the same stacks of language models are employed in the embedding layer and the Flair(forward+backward)+FastText+Character stack performed better than the other stacks again, showing that this combination of embeddings is very powerful for Bulgarian sequence tagging tasks.

Table 1 shows a summary of the previous systems with reported results for Bulgarian POS tagging, extending Table 5 from (Georgiev et al., 2009) with the experiments done after the publishing of the paper. Most of the systems before

2015 are concentrated on experiments for reducing the complexity of the morphosyntactic tagset which for Bulgarian consists of 680 tags.

In my experiments I am using the Universal Dependency version of BulTreeBank produced by (Osenova and Simov, 2015). Thus, I use the 16 tags of Universal POS tagset. The dataset can be downloaded at `https://github.com/UniversalDependencies/UD_Bulgarian-BTB`.

Tag	Num	Acc	Tag	Num	Acc.
NOUN	34,152	99.82	**ADV**	6,558	95.72
ADP	22,097	99.82	**CONJ**	4,860	99
PUNCT	22,058	100	**DET**	2,433	92.86
VERB	17,185	98.38	**NUM**	2,106	94.74
ADJ	13,591	96.57	**PART**	2,052	98.9
PRON	10,094	97.79	**SCONJ**	1,606	99.36
AUX	8,777	93	**INTJ**	143	98.64
PROPN	8,435	96.14	**X**	2	100

Table 4: Frequency of the universal tags in the Treebank. 156,149 tokens total. Column **Tag** contains the Universal POS tag, **Num** represent the number of occurrences, **Acc.** contains the per tag accuracy in %.

Table 4 represents the frequency of the tags within the data and the best accuracy for them achieved by my experiments. It is clear from the results that the main word categories expressing events and relations in text — verbs and nouns — are very well tagged — more than 98 % and 99 % respectively.

Two experiments were performed. In **experiment 1** are used the following embeddings: `bg-forward-fast` + `bg-backward-fast` + `Character embeddings` + `FastText`. The overall accuracy is 98.9 %. In **experiment 2** the embeddings used are: `bg-forward` + `bg-backward` + `Character embeddings` + `FastText` with overall accuracy 99.1 %.

4 Conclusions and Future Work

In these experiments are explored some combinations of the state-of-the-art embeddings on the NERC and POS tagging tasks for Bulgarian. The stack of Flair contextual string embeddings, FastText word embeddings, and Character embeddings outperformed all other combinations reported here.

The results are encouraging and the experiments will continue with training of custom contextual embeddings for Bulgarian and fine-tune them on the different tasks. The idea of solving several tasks simultaneously in a combined model like (Simova et al., 2014) and (Zhikov et al., 2013) is interesting too. The authors of these articles suggest that several tasks can be solved by one model without much damage to the individual scores, and it is interesting to explore the idea further. Moreover, it combines tasks similar to the classification of NE, events and relations, which is the aim of my PhD.

5   Acknowledgements

This research was partially supported by *the Bulgarian National Interdisciplinary Research e-Infrastructure for Resources and Technologies in favor of the Bulgarian Language and Cultural Heritage, part of the EU infrastructures CLARIN and DARIAH – CLaDA-BG*, Grant number DO01-164/28.08.2018.

References

Alan Akbik, Tanja Bergmann, Duncan Blythe, Kashif Rasul, Stefan Schweter, and Roland Vollgraf. 2019a. Flair: An easy-to-use framework for state-of-the-art nlp. In *Proceedings of the 2019 Conference of the North American Chapter of the Association for Computational Linguistics (Demonstrations)*. pages 54–59.

Alan Akbik, Tanja Bergmann, and Roland Vollgraf. 2019b. Pooled contextualized embeddings for named entity recognition. In *NAACL 2019, 2019 Annual Conference of the North American Chapter of the Association for Computational Linguistics*. page 724–728.

Alan Akbik, Duncan Blythe, and Roland Vollgraf. 2018. Contextual string embeddings for sequence labeling. In *Proceedings of the 27th International Conference on Computational Linguistics*. pages 1638–1649.

Piotr Bojanowski, Edouard Grave, Armand Joulin, and Tomas Mikolov. 2017. Enriching word vectors with subword information. *Transactions of the Association for Computational Linguistics* 5:135–146.

Jacob Devlin, Ming-Wei Chang, Kenton Lee, and Kristina Toutanova. 2018. Bert: Pre-training of deep bidirectional transformers for language understanding. *arXiv preprint arXiv:1810.04805* .

Georgi Georgiev, Preslav Nakov, Kuzman Ganchev, Petya Osenova, and Kiril Simov. 2009. Feature-rich named entity recognition for bulgarian using conditional random fields. In *Proceedings of the International Conference RANLP-2009*. pages 113–117.

Georgi Georgiev, Valentin Zhikov, Petya Osenova, Kiril Simov, and Preslav Nakov. 2012. Feature-rich part-of-speech tagging for morphologically complex languages: Application to bulgarian. In *Proceedings of the 13th Conference of the European Chapter of the Association for Computational Linguistics*. Association for Computational Linguistics, Stroudsburg, PA, USA, EACL '12, pages 492–502. http://dl.acm.org/citation.cfm?id=2380816.2380876.

Edouard Grave, Piotr Bojanowski, Prakhar Gupta, Armand Joulin, and Tomas Mikolov. 2018. Learning word vectors for 157 languages. In *Proceedings of the International Conference on Language Resources and Evaluation (LREC 2018)*.

Zhiheng Huang, Wei Xu, and Kai Yu. 2015. Bidirectional lstm-crf models for sequence tagging. *arXiv preprint arXiv:1508.01991* .

Tomas Mikolov, Ilya Sutskever, Kai Chen, Greg S Corrado, and Jeff Dean. 2013. Distributed representations of words and phrases and their compositionality. In *Advances in neural information processing systems*. pages 3111–3119.

Petya Osenova and Kiril Simov. 2015. Universalizing BulTreeBank: a linguistic tale about glocalization. In *The 5th Workshop on Balto-Slavic Natural Language Processing*. INCOMA Ltd. Shoumen, BULGARIA, Hissar, Bulgaria, pages 81–89. https://www.aclweb.org/anthology/W15-5313.

Jeffrey Pennington, Richard Socher, and Christopher Manning. 2014. Glove: Global vectors for word representation. In *Proceedings of the 2014 conference on empirical methods in natural language processing (EMNLP)*. pages 1532–1543.

Matthew E. Peters, Mark Neumann, Mohit Iyyer, Matt Gardner, Christopher Clark, Kenton Lee, and Luke Zettlemoyer. 2018. Deep contextualized word representations. In *Proc. of NAACL*.

Jakub Piskorski, Laska Laskova, Michał Marcińczuk, Lidia Pivovarova, Pavel Přibáň, Josef Steinberger, and Roman Yangarber. 2019. The second cross-lingual challenge on recognition, normalization, classification, and linking of named entities across Slavic languages. In *Proceedings of the 7th Workshop on Balto-Slavic Natural Language Processing*. Association for Computational Linguistics, Florence, Italy, pages 63–74. https://www.aclweb.org/anthology/W19-3709.

Barbara Plank, Anders Søgaard, and Yoav Goldberg. 2016. Multilingual part-of-speech tagging with bidirectional long short-term memory models and auxiliary loss. *arXiv preprint arXiv:1604.05529* .

Alexander Popov. 2016. Deep learning architecture for part-of-speech tagging with word and suffix embeddings. In Christo Dichev and Gennady Agre, editors, *Artificial Intelligence: Methodology, Systems, and Applications*. Springer International Publishing, Cham, pages 68–77.

Aleksandar Savkov, Laska Laskova, Petya Osenova, Kiril Simov, and Stanislava Kancheva. 2011. A web-based morphological tagger for bulgarian. *Slovko* pages 126–137.

Lilia Simeonova, Kiril Simov, Petya Osenova, and Preslav Nakov. 2019. A morpho-syntactically informed lstm-crf model for named entity recognition. In *Proceedings of the International Conference Recent Advances in Natural Language Processing 2019*. Association for Computational Linguistics, page in print.

Kiril Simov and Petya Osenova. 2001. A hybrid system for morphosyntactic disambiguation in bulgarian. In *Proceedings of the EuroConference on Recent Advances in Natural Language Processing*. Citeseer, pages 5–7.

Kiril Simov and Petya Osenova. 2004. BTB-TR04: BulTreeBank morphosyntactic annotation of Bulgarian texts. Technical report, Technical Report BTB-TR04, Bulgarian Academy of Sciences.

Kiril Simov, Petya Osenova, Milena Slavcheva, Sia Kolkovska, Elisaveta Balabanova, Dimitar Doikoff, Krassimira Ivanova, Alexander Simov, and Milen Kouylekov. 2002. Building a linguistically interpreted corpus of bulgarian: the bultreebank. In *LREC*.

Iliana Simova, Dimitar Vasilev, Alexander Popov, Kiril Simov, and Petya Osenova. 2014. Joint Ensemble Model for POS Tagging and Dependency Parsing. In *Proceedings of the First Joint Workshop on Statistical Parsing of Morphologically Rich Languages and Syntactic Analysis of Non-Canonical Languages*. Dublin City University, pages 15–25.

Erik F Tjong Kim Sang and Fien De Meulder. 2003. Introduction to the conll-2003 shared task: Language-independent named entity recognition. *arXiv preprint cs/0306050* .

Michihiro Yasunaga, Jungo Kasai, and Dragomir R. Radev. 2017. Robust multilingual part-of-speech tagging via adversarial training. *CoRR* abs/1711.04903. http://arxiv.org/abs/1711.04903.

Xiang Yu, Agnieszka Falenska, and Ngoc Thang Vu 2017. A general-purpose tagger with convolutional neural networks. *CoRR* abs/1706.01723. http://arxiv.org/abs/1706.01723.

Valentin Zhikov, Georgi Georgiev, Kiril Simov, and Petya Osenova. 2013. Combining POS Tagging, Dependency Parsing and Coreferential Resolution for Bulgarian. In *Proceedings of the International Conference Recent Advances in Natural Language Processing RANLP 2013*. pages 755–762.

Overview on NLP Techniques for Content-Based Recommender Systems for Books

Melania Berbatova
Sofia University "St. Kliment Ohridski"
melania.berbatova@uni-sofia.bg

Abstract

Recommender systems are an essential part of today's largest websites. Without them, it would be hard for users to find the right products and content. One of the most popular methods for recommendations is content-based filtering. It relies on analysing product metadata, a great part of which is textual data. Despite their frequent use, there is still no standard procedure for developing and evaluating content-based recommenders. In this paper, we first examine current approaches for designing, training and evaluating recommender systems based on textual data for books recommendations for the GoodReads website. We examine critically existing methods and suggest how natural language techniques could be employed for the improvement of content-based recommenders.

Nomenclature

CBF Content-based filtering

CF Collaborative filtering

RS Recommender systems

1   Introduction

Recommendation systems are engines that use algorithms leveraging the interaction between users to generate personalized recommendations. They provide users with recommendations for new content these users might be interested in (music, movies, books, etc).

Recommendation systems can be divided into three main types: Collaborative Filtering (CF), Content-based Filtering (CBF) and Hybrid systems. Collaborative filtering systems analyze users interactions with the items (e.g. through ratings, likes or clicks) to create recommendations.

On the other hand, content-based systems use semantic information (frequently called metadata) about the items in the system. Hybrid systems are a combination of these two approaches. If compared to collaborative or content-based systems, hybrid ones usually exhibit higher recommendation accuracy. This is due to the fact that CF lacks information about domain dependencies, while CBF systems do not take into account users preferences.(Krasnoshchok and Lamo, 2014)

Collaborative filtering recommenders are systems that suggest recommendations based on users interactions (most commonly, ratings). A great deal of the most efficient collaborative filtering algorithms are based on the matrix factorization (MF). Matrix factorization algorithms work by decomposing the user-item interaction matrix into the product of two lower dimensionality rectangular matrices. (Koren et al., 2009) This family of methods gained popularity around the Netflix prize challenge and showed state-of-art results for many RS tasks. However, in this paper we will focus on content-based methods, as they can benefit from natural language techniques and increase the accuracy of recommendations in a hybrid approach.

Content-based recommenders are a type of recommender systems that use item metadata (description, rating, products features, reviews, tags, genres) to find items, similar to those the user has enjoyed in the past. To generate recommendations, we use items that are most similar to the ones liked by a given user. In the context of books, main characteristics, and even whole book content can be present as metadata. As descriptions and reviews are purely natural language data, and categorical data such as tags and genres can also be represented in a way suitable for natural language processing, employing such techniques is crucial for the design of successful content-based recom-

55

Proceedings of the Student Research Workshop associated with RANLP-2019, pages 55–61,
Varna, Bulgaria, Sep 2–4, 2019.
https://doi.org/10.26615/issn.2603-2821.2019_009

menders.

In content-based recommendation systems, the features of products, e.g. the genre and the author of a book, are represented most often as a bag of words or a vector space model. Features of a book might refer to its title, summary, outline, whole text, or metadata, including the author, year of publication, publisher, genre, number of pages, etc.

Content-based recommenders use a variety of machine-learning algorithms, including Naive Bayes, support vector machines, decision trees, and kNN. As bag-of-words and vector representations can have hundreds or thousands of dimensions, techniques as Latent Dirichlet Allocation (LDA) are often adopted. The content may also require natural language processing (NLP) techniques to make use of semantic and syntactic characteristics.

A recommender system should not be designed without taking into consideration the nature of the items. Contrary to those of other text-based items, such as news and scientific papers, book preferences are highly influenced by characteristics specific to books, such as book size, readability level and writing style. Thes particularities motivate the designing of recommenders that perform both a syntactic and a semantic analysis of book texts. A promising way to enrich book metadata is the automatic genre identification. Users on community-based book websites can assign tags and organize books under custom-defined "shelves". These tags and shelves can serve as genres and can be used to indicate patterns in users' opinions.

2 Dataset

Goodbooks-10k is a compilation of 5,976,479 ratings for the most popular 10,000 books in the book website Goodreads, as well as book metadata for each book. The dataset is available online on the FastML website[1] . Data, in the form of ratings, books metadata, to-read tags, and user tags and shelves, is organised in 5 files. The distribution of ratings in this dataset is centered around 100 ratings per user, where the average rating per user is 4. The distribution of the number of ratings per user and the average rating per user seems to follow a multivariate normal distribution. (Greenquist et al., 2019)

[1] http://fastml.com/goodbooks-10k-a-new-dataset-for-book-recommendations/

Some previous research on the topic of books recommender systems relies on datasets such as Book-Crossing, LitRec (Vaz et al.), LibraryThing (Lu et al., 2010). The main advantage of the goodbooks-10k dataset over the above mentioned ones is the volume of data. As the number of records is close to 6 million and the data presented is diverse and consistent, it allows experimenting with different algorithms, including ones that are designed for big data.

3 Related Work

In their paper "A survey of book recommender systems", Alharthi et al. (2017) present a detailed survey on different approaches to book recommendation, compiled from over 30 papers up to 2017. These publications report results from CBF, CF and other methods obtained on the Book-Crossing, LitRec, LibraryThing, INEX, and Amazon reviews datasets. Only LitRec (Vaz et al.) dataset uses data from GoodReads.

In the current study, we will focus on models for GoodReads built on the goodbooks-10k dataset. Recent publications written on this dataset mostly deal with collaborative filtering. Out of 11 unique papers in English on recommender systems retrieved by Google Scholar when search is performed for goodbooks-10k (Le, 2019; Kula, 2017; Recommendation; Greenquist et al., 2019; Zhang et al., 2019, 2018; Paudel et al., 2018; Khanom et al., 2019; Kouris et al., 2018; Yang et al., 2018; Hiranandani et al., 2019), 10 examine algorithms for Collaborative filtering, two (Le, 2019; Greenquist et al., 2019) implement hybrid systems, and only one (Le, 2019) implement a simple content-based recommender. We will examine the content-based systems or components of hybrid systems, developed on goodbooks-10k, and will compare them to systems using another dataset for GoodReads - LitRec.

3.1 Overview

An overview of published content-based approaches for GoodReads is shown in Table 1.

In their bachelor thesis, Le (2019) implement simple collaborative, content-based and hybrid systems for book recommendations. Their content-based recommender uses only ratings data and leaves aside books metadata. They achieve a best score of 0.842 of root-mean-square error (RMSE) for FunkSVD algorithm.

Authors	Dataset	Features	Evaluation metrics	Algorithms	Dataset creation
Le (2019)	goodbooks-10k	ratings	MAP, CC, MPS, MNS, MDS	cosine similarity	test set - of 5-star ratings
Greenquist et al. (2019)	goodbooks-10k	tf-idf vectors	RMSE	cosine similarity	5+ ratings per user
(Alharthi and Inkpen, 2019)	Litrec	linguistic and stylometry features	precision@10, recall@10	kNN	10+ rating per user

Table 1: Overview of recent published papers

Greenquist et al. (2019) implement a CBF/CF hybrid system. To gather more information, they merge goodbooks-10k data with Amazon reviews data. For books representations, they use tf-idf vectors of the books descriptions, tags, and shelves. Authors report using book descriptions in their content-based approach, but it is unclear how they obtained the descriptions, as the latter are not present in the goodbooks-10k dataset.

In addition to published ones, there are many other approaches to the goodbook-10k dataset, implemented and shared by community members on platforms such as Kaggle.com. On Kaggles goodbook-10k dataset page, there are 31 shared kernels[2]. Some of them contain demonstrations on the development of content-based systems, including ones that use tags information. It can be seen that, as mentioned in (Greenquist et al., 2019), tags are turned into tf-idf vectors, and cosine similarity is used for determining the books that are the most similar to a given one.

Alharthi and Inkpen (2019) use the Litrec dataset to develop a book recommendation system based on the linguistic features of the books. Litrec dataset has ratings of 1,927 users of 3,710 literary books and contains the complete text of books tagged with part-of-speech labels.

The content-based systems that Alharthi and Inkpen develop are based on the analysis of lexical, character-based, syntactic, characterization and style features of the books texts. Feature sets are learned from book texts converted into a numerical value using one-hot encoding.

For linguistics analysis, the authors use Linguistic Inquiry and Word Count (LIWC) (Tausczik and Pennebaker, 2010), which is a popular resource that focuses on grammatical, content and psychological word categories. Using LIWC 2015 dictionary, Alharthi and Inkpen compute 94 categories, such as: percent of latinate words, function words, affect words, social words, perpetual processes etc.

Other text measurements are computed by using GutenTags built-in tagger (Brooke et al., 2015), which uses a stylistic lexicon to calculate stylistic aspects usually considered when analyzing English literature. The six styles are colloquial (informal) vs. literary, concrete vs. abstract and subjective vs. objective. In addition, they use the fiction-aware named entity recognizer LitNER to identify number of characters and number of locations mentioned in a book. Finally, a text readability measurement is introduced, by calculating the Flesch reading ease score. All 120 features are used for finding most similar books using k-nearest neighbours (kNN) and Extreme Trees (ET) algorithms, and are tested against CBF baselines: LDA, LSI, VSM and Doc2vec. Both kNN and ET achieved higher scores than the baselines in both precision@10 (0.36 and 0.37, respectively) and recall@10 (0.17 for both).

Unfortunately, in goodbooks-10k, the book content is not available, and it would be extremely hard to gather and process this data. Therefore introducing stylometry and content features, as the ones mentioned above, would be impossible. The only suitable way of incorporating linguistic features would be by analyzing tags or by scraping books descriptions and reviews available at GoodReads.

[2]https://www.kaggle.com/zygmunt/goodbooks-10k/kernels

3.2 Critiques on Content-Based Recommenders

The main critique with regards to the systems developed on goodreads-10k is the lack of usage of textual data, such as tags available. Even in the cases where tags are used, no attention has been paid to the fact that most of the tags follow a hierarchical structure (eg, "biographical", "biographical-fiction", "biographical-memoir") and some have similar or equal meaning (e.g. "ya-dystopian", "young-adult-dystopian", "teen-dystopian", "dystopian", "antiutopian", "utopia-dystopia").

In order to deal with hierarchy, ambiguity and synonyms, some data normalization and natural language processing techniques could be adopted. Tf-idf vectorization is a common technique in text processing; however, it is arguable whether it is the most suitable way for vectorizing tags information, as their distribution does not necessarily follow the one of words in natural text.

Another observation is that the systems developed do not take advantage of the recent advances in machine learning algorithms, especially deep learning, despite the large volume of the data available.

3.3 General Critiques

One general critique on the observed publications is the lack of standardization in dataset preparation and of evaluation metrics usage. Firstly, some redefine a "like" as having a rating of at least 3 stars, while others dont provide a clear definition of a like. Secondly, some drop users having less than 5 ratings, others - less than 10, and yet others seem not to take out any users. And lastly, since the initial dataset does not come with established training and test sets, the way different researchers have performed the train/test split seem to diverge. All these three factors result in different datasets used by the researchers, and therefore, lead to non comparable results.

Another factor that makes the results non-comparable is the difference in evaluation metrics used. As it can be seen in Table 1, there is a huge variety of metrics, such as those that measure rating predictions (root mean squared error (RMSE)), ranking metrics (precision@k, recall@K, mean average precision (MAP)), metrics for coverage (catalog coverage (CC)), metrics for personalization, diversity and novelty. Without suitable, unified metrics, it would be impossible to credibly prove that the use of NLP techniques will significantly improve RS performance on the current task.

Since general dataset preparation and the choice of the evaluation metrics is a considerable topic, not central for this research proposal, we would like to leave it for future research.

4 Experiments

There are 5,976,479 ratings in our dataset. We chose the standard split of 80% percent of randomly sampled ratings for training data and 20% for test data, resulting in 4,781,183 train ratings and 1,195,296 test ratings. Because of the large volume of data, we preferred this method over multiple fold cross validation, as the cross validation would have slowed the work of the predictive algorithms.

As shown in Figure 1, the higher ratings significantly outnumber the lower ones. Therefore, we chose to define a like as a rating of 4 or more stars, instead of 3 or more, as defined in previous research. We estimated that this would lead to more balanced data and a better approximation of readers perception, which was further proved by our experiments.

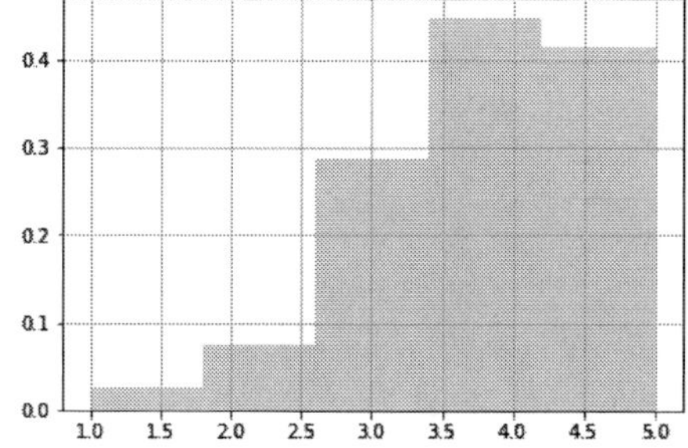

Figure 1: Distribution of ratings in the dataset

We used the python library TensorRec [3], which is a recommendation system library based on the deep learning library tensorflow, and employs the power of tensors and computational graphs. Recommender systems designed with TensorRec can be customized by choosing representation graphs, prediction graphs and loss graphs. Representation graphs are used for choosing the algorithms for latent representations (embeddings) of users and items. Prediction graphs are used for computing

---

[3] https://github.com/jfkirk/tensorrec

recommendation scores from the latent representations of users and items. Loss functions are the algorithms that define how loss is calculated from a set of recommendations.

We decided to work with recall@k as an evaluation metric. Recall@k shows the number of user's liked test items that were included in the top k of the predicted rankings, divided by k. Similar to Alharthi and Inkpen (2019), we chose k to be 10. We preferred recall@k than precision@k, because if the user has rated less than 10 books, precision@10 for their prediction cannot be 1. Finally, we preferred racall@k over RMSE and other metrics that measure the ratings prediction error, as for the design of the current recommender system, the exact score predicted is not as important as ranking the liked items higher than the not liked.

So far we have experimented with training simple CF and CBF systems. For our experiments, we used linear embeddings and weighted margin-rank batch (WMRB) (Liu and Natarajan, 2017) loss graph, which led to significantly better results on recall@10 than if optimizing for RMSE. For collaborative filtering we achieved 5.5% recall@10.

For the content-based approach, we used the year of publication and one-hot-encoded language as metadata features. We obtained results of 0.98% recall@10. The problem that we faced with content-based approach, was that we could not train algorithms with bigger feature sets, as there were memory errors when we ran our experiments both locally and in popular cloud services, such as CodeLab[4] and Kaggle[5]. This prevented us from evaluating the methods proposed in the current paper. The scores achieved by both methods with different parameters are shown in Table 2. As expected, approaches using ratings of 3 stars as a "like" showed worse results. We expect to improve results by several percents when we succeed in using more metadata features and we combine the designed CF and CBF in a hybrid system.

5 Suggested NLP Improvements

5.1 Using Tags Information

As we explained in the previous section, user tags information can be better utilized for the recommenders. The tags of a book show its genres (e.g. "young-adult", "fiction", "biography"), readers intents ("to-read", "to-buy", "to-be-finished"),

books features ("printed", "books-in-spanish"), awards ("printz-award"), authors ("oscar-wilde), etc. and many of the tags have similar or equal meanings. Every book is characterized by its tags and the number of occurrences of every tag. We dispose of almost 1 million tracks of (`(book_id, tag_id, count)`, or an average of 100 tags per book. The total number of defined tags is 34,251. Around 1000 of the tags are from languages different from English, such as Arabic, Persian, Russian, Greek etc. The set of tags per book is similar to textual data, except that there is no sequence between the tags.

We propose using a bag-of-words word model of tags, as being more suitable than a tf-idf-based one. Firstly, available tags need to be split into tokens and cleaned. Foreign language are around 3 percent of all, so excluding them is not expected to lead to significant loss of information. After cleaning and bag-of-words vectorization, we can extract a variety or features. As Alharthi and Inkpen (2019) mention, we can use linguistic resources as Linguistic Inquiry and Word Count, or alternatively, predefined dictionaries of book genres (such as the ones available on Wikipedia[6] and YourDictionary[7]) to design features of books genres and vocabulary style. The count of how many times the tokens of a book tags fall into a category can be used as a fuzzy representation of to what degree the given book belongs to a category. Alternatively, we can use the bag-of-words representations of tags together with an unsupervised dimensionality reduction algorithm, as latent semantic analysis (LSA), to represent books.

Another approach is to use the power of word embeddings. Embeddings are used for transforming a word into a vector from a vector space with a fixed dimensionality, in a way that words occurring in similar contexts are represented by similar vectors. Current pre-trained word embeddings, such as word2vec (Mikolov et al., 2013), ELMo (Peters et al., 2018) and BERT (Devlin et al., 2018) have proved to raise performance on many natural language processing tasks, including text classification (Lai et al., 2015). We can use the weighted average of the tags tokens of a book as representation of the book.

---

[4]https://codelabs.developers.google.com/
[5]https://www.kaggle.com/kernels

[6]https://en.wikipedia.org/wiki/List_of_writing_genres
[7]https://reference.yourdictionary.com/books-literature/different-types-of-books.html

Algorithm	Parameters	Recall@10
CF	Like = 3+ rating	4.69%
CF	Like = 4+ rating	5.52%
CBF	Like = 3+ rating	0.83%
CBF	Like = 4+ rating	0.98%

Table 2: Results

5.2 Data Enrichment

In addition to a better exploitation of the available data, we can also gather new natural language data and extract additional features from it. As mentioned by Greenquist et al. (2019), it would be useful to work with book descriptions. We can easily scrape these descriptions from GoodReads website using the books IDs, or, if unavailable in certain cases, we can scrape them from Amazon.com book pages. From descriptions we can extract features as sentiment and distribution of adjectives, adverbs, nouns, and verbs; or we can represent descriptions as tf-idf vectors.

5.3 Alternative Approaches

An alternative algorithmic approach to the ones discussed so far is to think of the recommendation task as a classification problem. For every user we can try to predict whether they "like" or "don't like" certain set of books, based on a training set of labeled books. In this setup, we can use books' metadata together with classical approaches for text classification, as SVM or Naive Bayes, or incorporate deep learning algorithms such as recurrent neural networks (RNNs) and long-short term memory (LSTM). If final predictions come with score for the labels given, we can sort the books in descending order of the scores for "like", take top 10 books in the sorted list and again measure recall@k. The downside of this approach is that it would not work well for users with too few ratings, as there will not be enough training data.

6 Conclusion

Many natural language processing techniques, such as extracting lexical, syntactic and stylometric features or word embeddings, can be used in content-based filtering for the recommendation of books. CBF systems employing these techniques can be used separately or in a hybrid with collaborative filtering. However, these techniques should be accompanied with standardized methods for dataset creation and result evaluation, so the results obtained are comparable to those from similar research.

References

Haifa Alharthi and Diana Inkpen. 2019. Study of linguistic features incorporated in a literary book recommender system. In *Proceedings of the 34th ACM/SIGAPP Symposium on Applied Computing*, pages 1027–1034. ACM.

Julian Brooke, Adam Hammond, and Graeme Hirst. 2015. Gutentag: an nlp-driven tool for digital humanities research in the project gutenberg corpus. In *Proceedings of the Fourth Workshop on Computational Linguistics for Literature*, pages 42–47.

Jacob Devlin, Ming-Wei Chang, Kenton Lee, and Kristina Toutanova. 2018. Bert: Pre-training of deep bidirectional transformers for language understanding. *arXiv preprint arXiv:1810.04805*.

Nicholas Greenquist, Doruk Kilitcioglu, and Anasse Bari. 2019. Gkb: A predictive analytics framework to generate online product recommendations. In *2019 IEEE 4th International Conference on Big Data Analytics (ICBDA)*, pages 414–419. IEEE.

Gaurush Hiranandani, Raghav Somani, Oluwasanmi Koyejo, and Sreangsu Acharyya. 2019. Clustered monotone transforms for rating factorization. In *Proceedings of the Twelfth ACM International Conference on Web Search and Data Mining*, pages 132–140. ACM.

Aniqa Zaida Khanom, Sheikh Mastura Farzana, Tahsinur Rahman, and Iftekharul Mobin. 2019. Bookception: A proposed framework for an artificially intelligent recommendation platform. In *Proceedings of the 2019 8th International Conference on Software and Computer Applications*, pages 253–257. ACM.

Yehuda Koren, Robert Bell, and Chris Volinsky. 2009. Matrix factorization techniques for recommender systems. *Computer*, (8):30–37.

Panagiotis Kouris, Iraklis Varlamis, Georgios Alexandridis, and Andreas Stafylopatis. 2018. A versatile package recommendation framework aiming at preference score maximization. *Evolving Systems*, pages 1–19.

Oleksandr Krasnoshchok and Yngve Lamo. 2014. Extended content-boosted matrix factorization algorithm for recommender systems. *Procedia Computer Science*, 35:417–426.

Maciej Kula. 2017. Mixture-of-tastes models for representing users with diverse interests. *arXiv preprint arXiv:1711.08379*.

Siwei Lai, Liheng Xu, Kang Liu, and Jun Zhao. 2015. Recurrent convolutional neural networks for text classification. In *Twenty-ninth AAAI conference on artificial intelligence*.

Hieu Le. 2019. Building and evaluating recommender systems.

Kuan Liu and Prem Natarajan. 2017. Wmrb: Learning to rank in a scalable batch training approach. *arXiv preprint arXiv:1711.04015*.

Caimei Lu, Jung-ran Park, and Xiaohua Hu. 2010. User tags versus expert-assigned subject terms: A comparison of librarything tags and library of congress subject headings. *Journal of information science*, 36(6):763–779.

Tomas Mikolov, Kai Chen, Greg Corrado, and Jeffrey Dean. 2013. Efficient estimation of word representations in vector space. *arXiv preprint arXiv:1301.3781*.

Bibek Paudel, Sandro Luck, and Abraham Bernstein. 2018. Loss aversion in recommender systems: Utilizing negative user preference to improve recommendation quality. *arXiv preprint arXiv:1812.11422*.

Matthew E Peters, Mark Neumann, Mohit Iyyer, Matt Gardner, Christopher Clark, Kenton Lee, and Luke Zettlemoyer. 2018. Deep contextualized word representations. *arXiv preprint arXiv:1802.05365*.

Collaborative-Filtering Recommendation. Building information systems using collaborative-filtering recommendation techniques. In *Advanced Information Systems Engineering Workshops: CAiSE 2019 International Workshops, Rome, Italy, June 3–7, 2019, Proceedings*, page 214. Springer.

Yla R Tausczik and James W Pennebaker. 2010. The psychological meaning of words: Liwc and computerized text analysis methods. *Journal of language and social psychology*, 29(1):24–54.

Paula Cristina Vaz, Ricardo Ribeiro, and David Martins de Matos. Litrec vs. movielens.

Fan Yang, Ninghao Liu, Suhang Wang, and Xia Hu. 2018. Towards interpretation of recommender systems with sorted explanation paths. In *2018 IEEE International Conference on Data Mining (ICDM)*, pages 667–676. IEEE.

Shuai Zhang, Lina Yao, Yi Tay, Xiwei Xu, Xiang Zhang, and Liming Zhu. 2018. Metric factorization: Recommendation beyond matrix factorization. *arXiv preprint arXiv:1802.04606*.

Xuejian Zhang, Zhongying Zhao, Chao Li, Yong Zhang, and Jianli Zhao. 2019. An interpretable and scalable recommendation method based on network embedding. *IEEE Access*, 7:9384–9394.

Corpora and Processing Tools for Non-Standard Contemporary and Diachronic Balkan Slavic

Teodora Vuković   Nora Muheim   Olivier Winistörfer
Ivan Šimko   Anastasia Makarova   Sanja Bradjan

Slavic Departement, University of Zurich, Plattenstrasse 43, Zurich
`teodora.vukovic2@uzh.ch`, `nora.muheim@uzh.ch`,
`olivier-andreas.winistoerfer@uzh.ch`, `ivan.simko@uzh.ch`,
`anastasia.makarova@uzh.ch`, `sanja.bradjan@uzh.ch`

Abstract

The paper describes three corpora of different varieties of BS that are currently being developed with the goal of providing data for the analysis of the diatopic and diachronic variation in non-standard Balkan Slavic. The corpora includes spoken materials from Torlak, Macedonian dialects, as well as the manuscripts of pre-standardized Bulgarian. Apart from the texts, tools for PoS annotation and lemmatization for all varieties are being created, as well as syntactic parsing for Torlak and Bulgarian varieties. The corpora are built using a unified methodology, relying on the pest practices and state-of-the-art methods from the field. The uniform methodology allows the contrastive analysis of the data from different varieties. The corpora under construction can be considered a crucial contribution to the linguistic research on the languages in the Balkans as they provide the lacking data needed for the studies of linguistic variation in the Balkan Slavic, and enable the comparison of the said varieties with other neighbouring languages.

1 Introduction

Balkan Slavic (BS) languages are the eastern branch of South Slavic languages, which are known for their affiliation to the so-called Balkansprachbund. The languages that belong to this group are Bulgarian and Macedonian varieties as well as the Torlak dialects spoken in South East Serbia and West Bulgaria. These languages express typological differences from other Slavic languages. Some of the differentiating features are: complete or almost complete loss of the noun case inflection and fully or partially grammaticalized post-positive definite articles (Lindstedt, 2000). Many other differences lie in the nominal and verbal morphosyntax, adjectival morphology, and tense and mood system, as well as in the lexical and phraseological domain. Nonetheless, the area itself is not linguistically uniform. On the contrary - the diversification starts from the division into official standard languages, further separated by various phonological and structural isoglosses (Ivić, 1985; Institute for Bulgarian Language, 2018; Stojkov, 2002; Vidoeski, 1999). Variation occurs even in very small regions, such as the Timok area in South East Serbia, where substantial differences occur in the use of post-posed articles between villages in the mountains and valleys or urban areas (Vuković and Samardžić, 2018). There is a significant variation not only from an areal, but also from a diachronic point of view. Looking at older texts written in pre-standardized Bulgarian, phases of change in the language happening over time are noticeable.

This variation is best analyzed in non-standard varieties, unaffected or minimally affected by the prescriptive standard, and ideally in the form of spoken language since it represents arguably a more "natural" state. In this paper, we present three ongoing projects on South Slavic dialectology and diachronic linguistics, which are currently being elaborated at the Slavic linguistics department at the University of Zurich. In these projects, special focus is on places in time and space where the change happens and the underlying grammatical processes and structures. Apart from linguistic questions, the focus of our research is on the identification of potential geographical and social factors influencing changes in Bulgarian, Torlak and Macedonian.

For the purpose of this research, we are aiming at three corpora (and also processing

Proceedings of the Student Research Workshop associated with RANLP-2019, pages 62–68,
Varna, Bulgaria, Sep 2–4, 2019.
https://doi.org/10.26615/issn.2603-2821.2019_010

tools) for modern and historical non-standard BS varieties that reflect diachronic and diatopic variation within the Balkan Slavic languages. The varieties covered are pre-standardized Bulgarian, Macedonian dialects, and Torlak varieties from Serbia and Bulgaria. Apart from the large collection of texts, the resources are equipped with part-of-speech (PoS) and morphosyntactic description (MSD) annotation, while some corpora also include a syntactic tree-bank and a layer of normalization. In order to make the corpora mutually comparable, we are developing and applying a uniform methodology. Methodology, corpora and tools are based on the existing standards used in the field as well as resources for the standard languages of the area, wherever available. This enables inter-comparability and reproducibility of the data. At the same time re-using already existing tools makes the process easier for the creators and it offers well-established methods too, which are discussed below.

2 Related Work

There is currently little data available in digital form that allows the analysis of the mentioned variation and change in BS. Bulgarian is the only language supplemented with a corpus of non-standard spoken varieties apart from the standard ones (Alexander, Ronelle and Zhobov, Vladimir, 2016; Alexander, 2015). Serbian only has corpora of written standard and computer-mediated communication (CMC) (CCSL; Utvić, 2011; Ljubešić and Klubička, 2014; Miličević and Ljubešić, 2016b). The only available searchable resource for Macedonian is an unannotated corpus of movie subtitles (Steinberger et al., 2014; Lison and Tiedemann, 2016). The mentioned corpora of standard language (or movie subtitles) are extremely valuable resources in itself, but they provide little-to-no insight into variation because they are a sample of only one variety by definition; furthermore, that standard-variety is by default controlled by people's prescribed conceptions of how language should be and how it should be written.

The only dialect corpus of BS, *Bulgarian Dialectology as Living Tradition* (Alexander, Ronelle and Zhobov, Vladimir, 2016; Alexander, 2015) is a database of oral speech comprising 184 texts from 69 Bulgarian villages, recorded between 1986 and 2013, and is 95,000 tokens in size. Texts were transcribed into Latin and Cyrillic script in order to make the data available to a wider audience. The texts are annotated with grammatical information, lemmas, English glosses for each token, and English translations for each line (see the annotated sentence in example 1, presented as it is in the corpus). The MSD are easily readable, but do not fin the standards used in the field. The database represents an impressive achievement, and a particularly valuable one given that it is the sole resource for dialectal research on BS at the moment.

(1)   *hm   kvó   se*
      disc what.Sg.N.Interr   Acc.Refl.Clt
      .   какво   це
      kázvaše
      say.3Sg.Impf.I
      казвам
      'Hmmmm. What is it called?'

The corpora described in this paper are created with the goal to be comparable with other existing related resources – be it corpora of dialects or of the standard language. The automatic processing tools developed for the language varieties included in the collection are created based on existing ones whenever possible. For example, the morphosyntactic tagger and lemmatizer for Torlak is an adaptation of the tagger for standard Serbian (Miličević and Ljubešić, 2016a).

An important tool for Serbian is the ReLDI tagger, which assigns morphosyntactic tags and lemmas to text (Ljubešić, 2016). The tagger was developed for standard Serbian, Croatian, and Slovene using a character-level machine translation method. It assigns tags specified by the MULTEXT-East standards (Krstev et al., 2004). The python package allows training for any other variety with an novel training set as an input (Ljubešić, 2016).

MULTEXT-East resources represent an extremely important milestone in the field of computational linguistic for South Slavic languages (Erjavec, 2010). The collection includes the manually annotated novel *1984* by George Orwell that can be used for training and testing of resources and specifications for morphosyntactic descriptions. The PoS labels are formulated as a string of characters, where each character stands for a grammatical category (e.g. the tag Ncfsn for the Serbian noun kuća, 'house', means 'Noun, common, feminine, singular, nominative').

The recently widely used convention of the Universal Dependencies (UD) database contains tools and specifications for the annotation of morphology and syntactic parsing for many languages, using universal grammatical categories founded in dependency grammar. The repository includes tree-banks and MSD taggers for the closely related South Slavic languages Serbian and Bulgarian.

3 Balkan Slavic Corpora

In order to bridge this gap and supply the materials necessary for the analysis of the multi-sided variation in BS, we are creating several spoken and historical corpora of varieties from the region, namely the territories in present-day Serbia, Bulgaria, and Macedonia. The individual corpora are presently at different stages of development. Contemporary materials have been collected in the past 10 years, while the historical data comprises some more recent 19th and 20th century resources that could be classified as micro-diachronical (representing a shorter time span), as well as older manuscripts dating from 16th-19th century, which provide a view on the language change on a larger scale. The goal is to establish a pipeline and tools that match the needs for non-standard varieties and produce comparable resources and would in turn allow the analysis of variation in a set of close languages.

3.1 Corpus Structure and Methodology

In order to make the corpora comparable among themselves but also with other corpora of neighboring languages, we are applying some standards from the field as well as creating them to fit a uniform structure. This will also result in ease of access and user-friendliness.

For texts which originate from audio recordings, transcripts have been made using Exmaralda (Schmidt, 2010) transcription software, developed specifically for linguistic transcription. The optical character recognition (OCR) for the printed texts and manuscripts was performed in Transkribus (Digitisation and Digital Preservation group, 2019), another piece of software created at the University of Innsbruck for automatic transcriptions of older texts and scripts.

Transcripts of spoken materials are segmented into utterances based on intonation or syntactic patterns, and each utterance is aligned with an interval on the recording. Texts that have been digitized from prints preserve the segmentation into sentences from the original version. Lastly, texts derived from written manuscripts, which do not always have clear sentence structure or punctuation, have been segmented into sentences in post-editing based syntactic structure and meaning.

Each corpus contains several layers. The minimum are the original text with automatically assigned PoS tags and lemmas, while some also contain some form of standardization or normalization. The structure of the corpus allows more information to be added over time (e.g. English glosses or an English translation).

When it comes to PoS and MSD annotation, the MULTEXT-East tag-set is used, because it is a widely accepted standard for morphologically complex languages of Eastern Europe. A further advantage is its easy adaptability to new grammatical categories, so the grammar of different varieties can be matched. We chose the MULTEXT-East tag-set over UD because they are mutually compatible. Namely, they both mark the same categories but in a different way (e.g. the MULTEXT-East tag 'Ncmsn' would be converted to the UD tag 'UPOS=NOUN, Case=Nom, Gender=Masc, Number=Sing'). They can be easily transformed from one to the other, and in fact, this has already been done for the Serbian UD Tree-bank (Samardžić et al., 2017).

All the corpora are provided with relevant metadata containing (where possible) age, gender, year of recording and main occupation of the informants as well as geo-spatial information about speaker locations. In the case of the pre-standardized Bulgarian corpus, the metadata base consists of approximate dating of the manuscripts and supposed location of its creation. The metadata for the dialectal Macedonian corpus is sometimes fragmentary because of the different working standards used and it is not possible to recover the lacking information. The metadata may be later used as a starting point for the analysis of the correlation of the linguistic data with non-linguistic factors.

The corpora are stored in files with XML markup in accordance with the TEI standards for spoken language and manuscripts (TEI, 2019). Aligned audio files are currently not supplemented with the recordings due to the lacking infrastructure. However, recordings can be accessed on the project's YouTube channel (TraCeBa, 2015). The corpora will be made available online and freely accessible.

Each corpus has been tailored to match the methodology described above. This way different samples can be searched at the same time and the results compared. The following subsections present individual corpora on various BS varieties.

3.2 Torlak Corpus

The contemporary section of the Torlak corpus is based on fieldwork recordings from the Timok and Lužnica regions in South-East Serbia, and areas around Belogradčik in Western Bulgaria. The interviews have been transcribed using Exmaralda (Schmidt, 2010). The micro-diachronic part of the corpus includes dialect transcripts form East Serbia and West Bulgaria (Sobolev, 1998) collected by Andrey N. Sobolev in the 1990s, which have been digitized from the printed version using Transkribus (Digitisation and Digital Preservation group, 2019) as well as the data collected in the beginning of the 20th century by Belić (Belić, 1905) and Stanojević (Stanojević, 1911). Two parts of the collection have been completed so far. The collection from Timok contains around 350,000 tokens and the one from the 1990s has close to 100,000 tokens. The other data is currently being transcribed and will contain in total roughly 200,000 tokens.

Semi-phonetic transcription of spoken data have been made to reflect the spoken language as well as possible while maintaining a necessary level of readability. The transcripts of audio recordings and those of the printed interviews contain information about the accent position encoded in capital letters. They also include information about interruptions and overlaps, which is not available for the interviews recovered from print.

We have developed a PoS tagger and a lemmatizer for the contemporary spoken data from Timok and Lužnica using the ReLDI model. The training data and the lexicon combines Serbian and dialect material. For the Serbian part we used the SETTimes reference training corpus (Batanović, 2018) and the lexicon SrLex 1.2 (Ljubešić and Jazbec, 2016), both freely available. The dialect part consists of the 20,000 tokens, which have been pre-annotated with the ReLDI tagger, and then manually corrected and the lexicon derived

from that sample. The accuracy of the tagger on the data Timok and Lužnica is 92.9% for the PoS labels and 93.9% for the lemmas. However, the accuracy is lower for the other sections of this corpus from the 1990s and earlier, and from Bulgaria. We are currently adding more manually annotated data from these sources to improve the results. An example of a sentence from the corpus annotated with MULTEXT-East PoS tags in the second line and lemmas in the third line is given in example 2.

(2) *On   došAl   sInoč   iz   zAjčar*
    Pp3msn   Vmp-sm   Rgp   Sg   Npmsa
    on   doći   sinoć   iz   Zaječar
    'He came last night from Zaječar.'

Apart from the morphological annotations, we are presently developing a UD-based tree-bank using the labels from the Serbian UD treebank (Samardžić et al., 2017). The data has been pre-annotated with the parser for Serbian and is being manually corrected in Arborator (Gerdes, 2013).

3.3 Macedonian Dialect Corpus

The goal in this project is to create the first corpus of spoken Macedonian dialects, annotated with PoS tags and with lemmatized tokens. The data is mainly drawn from transcripts of field-work interviews with older people from different locations collected by Vidoeski from the 1950s until the 1970s. This text-collection also includes interviews from other researchers besides Vidoeski, of which some work is considerably older than Vidoeski's; several interviews are even dating back to 1892. All the texts have been published by Vidoeski 1999. The covered period of time gives the corpus a certain diachronic depth. The texts have been transcribed using Transkribus (Digitisation and Digital Preservation group, 2019). The modern state of Western Macedonian dialects is presented by the recent field data from multi-ethnic Ohrid, Prespa, Struga and Debar regions collected in 2013 - 2019 (Makarova, 2019). The contemporary data allows a contrastive analysis of the hypothesized change.

The data comes from diverse origins, so a unified metadata scheme cannot be applied to all the collections. As these interviews were not planned as one project, every researcher defined their own standard. To partially solve this challenge and guarantee some uniformity, a standardized frame is used, where potential gaps are clearly stated.

This allows the user to decide for themselves which amount of background information is enough (e.g. if they accept an unclear year of recording or no information about the speaker's sex) and whether they want to include such parts of the corpus with missing information in their research or not.

There are currently practically no automatic tools that could be used to do PoS annotation for dialectal Macedonian, so they need to be developed specifically for this corpus. The only previous attempt to produce an automatic tagger for Macedonian has been done by Aepli et al.2014, where they solely used part-of-speech categories with no morphology at all. In our approach, we will use the MULTEXT-East tag-set for Macedonian with minor modifications to accommodate the dialectal categories not present in the standard (such as nominal cases for instance) and the ReLDI tagger. To train the initial model we will use the manually annotated corpus and the lexicon provided in the MULTEXT-East collection for standard Macedonian. After the initial training with this material we will correct the results to take the dialectal forms and variations into account. The manually annotated sample will then be used to train a new model, suitable for the many dialects covered by the corpus. The following example shows one manually annotated sentence from the contemporary material (Makarova, 2019):

(3)   ***Pominav***   ***mnogu***   ***ubo***   ***detstvo***.
      Vmia1s-anp   Rgp   Rgp   Ncnsnn
      pomine   mnogu   ubavo   detstvo
      'I remember a lot from childhood.'

3.4 Pre-Standardized Bulgarian

The corpus for pre-standardized Bulgarian contains texts from the period between the 16th and 19th century, mostly, but not exclusively from present-day Bulgaria. The texts are chosen according to the similarity of their language and the vernacular. Thus, Church Slavonic texts were generally avoided, but some of them were added for reference. The collection includes texts from the Damaskini tradition either as a whole (Kotel, Ljubljana, Loveč, Tixonravov and Svištov damaskini, Pop Punčo's miscellany, perspectively also manuscript NBKM 328 of Iosif Bradati), or as a parallel corpus of multiple versions of a recurring story, (e.g. *Life of St Petka*, *Second Coming of Christ* or multiple transcripts of the *Slavobulgarian Chronicle* by Paisius of Hilandar).

Parallel corpora consisting of editions of the same text from various stages and dialectal or literary backgrounds, enable us to observe the development of linguistic features or orthographic influences independently of the differences caused by contents and genre. The manuscripts have been digitized from the printed or handwritten versions using Transkribus (Digitisation and Digital Preservation group, 2019).

The MSD labels are based on the MULTEXT-East specifications for Modern Bulgarian. The purpose of this corpus is to provide material for the study of the changes in the morphosyntactic features between Middle and Modern Bulgarian. This makes the the standardized Bulgarian tag-set unsuitable. To overcome instances of ambiguity within a text and within the corpus, we adapted it to reflect both archaic and innovative features. These include nominal case markers (e.g. dative and genitive-accusative being regularly marked on both masculine nouns and adjectives), verbal infinitives (e.g. *koi može iskaza* 'who could retell') and multiple options to mark the definiteness (short- and long-forms of the adjective, articles tagged as separate tokens). Phonetic ambiguities (e.g. /i/ and /y/) were resolved by conventions based on the development of the sound in the approximate area of origin of the text. In order to avoid any over-interpretation or bias, the tags used for cases refer to morphological and not syntactical (e.g. verbal voice) or semantic (e.g. difference between common and proper nouns) criteria.

The literature of this period inherited the complex orthography of Church Slavonic. Already in the Middle Bulgarian period, it was the case that many of its rules were obsolete. Both Church Slavonic and vernacular literature attempted to follow these rules, but they weren't applied consequently. In the end, the same lemma may appear with different spellings, sometimes even within the same sentence. The different manifestations of the same lemma were partly unified by using a diplomatic transcription, eliminating ambiguous signs (e.g. accents, writing of /i/). Furthermore they were unified under the lemmas of the dictionary based on Tixonravov Damaskin, see (Demina, 2012). Turkish loanwords, Church Slavonicisms, and Russian words not included in this dictionary were lemmatized with the Etymological dictionary of BAN (Georgiev, 2006; Todorov, 2002) or with

Church Slavonic dictionaries, e.g. (Cejtlin, 1994).

The first instance of the PoS tagger and the lemmatizer was trained on a sample of 6000 manually annotated tokens using the ReLDI framework (Ljubešić, 2016). Given the unsatisfactory accuracy, we are in the process of adding more manually annotated training data. A sample of an annotated sentence from the corpus is given in the example 4. At the same time we are working on a UD-style tree-bank using syntactic labels taken from Bulgarian and Serbian specifications (Samardžić et al., 2017; Osenova and Simov, 2004).

(4) ***Prědade+ sŷ dšá+ ta bu.***
Vmia3s Px—d Nfsnn Pa-fsn Nmsdy
prědam se duša ta bog
'He surrendered his soul to the God.'

4   Conclusion

In joining our work on different languages with similar challenges, we are able to show how to deal with variation in corpora in a principled way and therefore contribute to the field of dialectology, on the one hand, and corpus linguistics on the other. Secondly, our approach demonstrates the fruitfulness of combining methodology for multiple similar projects, by taking advantage of the best practices and state-of-the-art methods and tools. The unified methodology in turn guarantees comparability of the data, which is required for the analysis of change and variation in several different varieties. The corpora under construction in the context of our projects can be considered a significant contribution to the linguistic research on the languages in the Balkans as they provide the lacking data needed for linguistic studies of BS, as well as comparison of the mentioned varieties with other neighbouring languages.

The output of these projects will be the corpora of spoken and written non-standard language equipped with with PoS annotation and lemmatization, as well as UD tree-banks. Additionally, the tools for automatic processing will be available for re-use, as well as training data and lexicons developed based on them. All of the resources will be made available online.

Acknowledgments

The development of the resources described in the paper has been funded by various sources: TraCeBa project (EraNet Rus Plus grant/Swiss National Science Foundation IZRPZ0_177557/1), Ill-bred sons project (Swiss National Science Foundation 100015_176378/1, Swiss Excellence Government Scholarship awarded to Teodora Vuković and Anastasia Makarova, Language and Space UZH, SyNoDe UZH, Slavisches Seminar UZH, Doctoral Program Linguistics UZH and Ministry of Culture and Information of Serbia. We would like to express our gratitude for their support.

References

Aepli, N., von Waldenfels, R., and Samardžić, T. (2014). Part-of-speech tag disambiguation by cross-linguistic majority vote. In *Proceedings of the First Workshop on Applying NLP Tools to Similar Languages, Varieties and Dialects*, pages 76–84.

Alexander, R. (2015). Bulgarian dialectology as living tradition: A digital resource of dialectal speech. pages 1–13.

Alexander, Ronelle and Zhobov, Vladimir (2016). Bulgarian dialectology as living tradition.

Batanović, Vuk; Ljubešić, N. S. T. (2018). Setimes.sr — a reference training corpus of serbian. pages 11––17, Ljubljana, Slovenia.

Belić, A. (1905). *Dijalekti istočne i južne Srbije*. Srpski dijalektološki zbornik. Sprska Kraljevska Akademija.

Cejtlin, Ralja Večerka; Radoslav Blagova, E. (1994). *Staroslavjanskij slovar: po rukopisjam X-XI vekov*. Russkij jazyk, Moskva.

Demina, Evgenia Mičeva; Vania Seizova, S. (2012). *Rečnik na knižovnija bălgarski ezik na narodna osnova ot XVII vek*. Valentin Trajanov, Sofia.

Digitisation and Digital Preservation group (2019). Transkribus. https://transkribus.eu/ Transkribus/. [Online; accessed 09-July-2019].

Erjavec, T. (2010). Multext-east version 4 : multilingual morphosyntactic specifications, lexicons and corpora. In *V: Proceedings, LREC 2010, 7th International Conference on Language Resources and Evaluations*, pages 2544–2547.

Georgiev, V. (1972–2006). *Bălgarski etimologičen rečnik I-V*. Marin Drinov, Sofia.

Gerdes, K. (2013). Collaborative dependency annotation. In *Proceedings of the Second International Conference on Dependency Linguistics (DepLing 2013)*, Prague, Czech Republic. Charles University in Prague, Matfyzpress, Prague, Czech Republic.

Institute for Bulgarian Language (2018). Map of the dialectal division of the bulgarian language. `http://ibl.bas.bg/bulgarian_dialects/`. [Online; accessed 05-July-2018].

Ivić, P. (1985). *Dijalektologija srpskohrvatskog jezika: Uvod i štokavsko narečje.* Matica srpska, Novi Sad.

Krstev, C., Vitas, D., and Erjavec, T. (2004). Morpho-Syntactic Descriptions in MULTEXT-East - the Case of Serbian. *Informatica, No. 28.*

Lindstedt, J. (2000). Linguistic balkanization: Contact-induced change by mutual reinforcement. In Gilbers, D., editor, *Languages in contact.* number 28 in Studies in Slavic and general linguistics. Rodopi, Amsterdam.

Lison, P. and Tiedemann, J. (2016). Opensubtitles2016: Extracting large parallel corpora from movie and tv subtitles. In *Proceedings of the 10th International Conference on Language Resources and Evaluation (LREC 2016).* European Language Resources Association (ELRA).

Ljubešić, Nikola; Klubička, F. A. Z. and Jazbec, I.-P. (2016). New inflectional lexicons and training corpora for improved morphosyntactic annotation of croatian and serbian. In *Proceedings of the Tenth International Conference on Language Resources and Evaluation (LREC 2016).*

Ljubešić, Nikola; Klubička, F. A. Z. J. I.-P. (2016). New inflectional lexicons and training corpora for improved morphosyntactic annotation of croatian and serbian. In Calzolari, N., Choukri, K., Declerck, T., Goggi, S., Grobelnik, M., Maegaard, B., Mariani, J., Mazo, H., Moreno, A., Odijk, J., and Piperidis, S., editors, *Proceedings of the Tenth International Conference on Language Resources and Evaluation (LREC'16)*, Portorož. European Language Resources Association (ELRA).

Ljubešić, Nikola; Klubička, F. A. Z. J. I.-P. (2016). New inflectional lexicons and training corpora for improved morphosyntactic annotation of croatian and serbian. In Chair), N. C. C., Choukri, K., Declerck, T., Goggi, S., Grobelnik, M., Maegaard, B., Mariani, J., Mazo, H., Moreno, A., Odijk, J., and Piperidis, S., editors, *Proceedings of the Tenth International Conference on Language Resources and Evaluation (LREC 2016)*, Paris, France. European Language Resources Association (ELRA).

Ljubešić, N. and Klubička, F. (2014). Wac – web corpora of bosnian, croatian and serbian. In *Proceedings of the 9th Web as Corpus Workshop (WaC-9)*, pages 29—35.

Makarova, A. (2019). Unpublished work.

Miličević, M. and Ljubešić, N. (2016a). Tviterasi, tviteraši or twitteraši? producing and analysing a normalised dataset of croatian and serbian tweets. *Slovenščina 2.0*, 4(2):156–188.

Miličević, M. and Ljubešić. N. (2016b). *Tviterasi, tviteraši or twitteraši? Producing and analysing a normalised dataset of Croatian and Serbian tweets.* Slovenščina 2.0.

Osenova, P. and Simov, K. (2004). Btb-tr05: Bultreebank stylebook 05. Technical report.

Samardžić, T., Starović, M., Agić, v., and Ljubešić, N. (2017). Universal dependencies for serbian in comparison with croatian and other slavic languages. In *Proceedings of the 6th Workshop on Balto-Slavic Natural Language Processing*, pages 39–44, Valencia, Spain. Association for Computational Linguistics.

Schmidt, T. (2010). Exmaralda: un systéme pour la constitution et l'exploitation de corpus oraux. *Pour une épistémologie de la sociolinguistique. Actes du colloque international de Montpellier*, pages 319–327.

Sobolev, A. (1998). *Sprachatlas Ostserbiens und Westbulgariens.* Scripta Slavica. Biblion.

Stanojević, M. (1911). *Severno-timački dijalekat.* Dijalektološki zbornik. Sprska Akademija Nauka.

Steinberger, R., Ebrahim, M., Poulis, A., Carrasco-Benitez. M., Schlüter, P., Przybyszewski, M., and Gilbro, S. (2014). An overview of the european union's highly multilingual parallel corpora. *Language resources and evaluation*, pages 679–707.

Stojkov, S. (2002). *Bălgarska dialektologija.* Akad. izd. Prof. Marin Drinov, Sofia.

TEI, T. E. I. (2019). *P5: Guidelines for Electronic Text Encoding and Interchange.*

CCSL. Corpus of contemporary serbian language - official website (in serbian). `http://www.korpus.matf.bg.ac.rs/prezentacija/istorija.html`. [Online; accessed 08-March-2018].

Todorov, T. A., editor (2002). *Bălgarski etimologičen rečnik VI-VII.* Sofia.

TraCeBa (2015). Terenska istrazivanja. `https://www.youtube.com/channel/UC4EpCSAnEb2RIsIRY7pfNdQ/feed`. [Online; accessed 20-August-2019].

Utvić, M. (2011). Anotacija korpusa savremenog srpskog jezika. *INFOteka 12, br. 2*, pages 39–51.

Vidoeski, B. (1999). *Dijalektite na Makedonskiot Jazik - tom 2.* MANU, Skopje.

Vuković, T. and Samardžić, T. (2018). Prostorna raspodela frekvencije postpozitivnog člana u timočkom govoru. In Ćirković, Svetlana (Ed. in chief) and Andrej N. Sobolev, Barbara Sonnenhauser, Maja Miličević, Jelenka Pandurević, editor, *Timok. Terenska istraživanja 2015--2017.* Narodna Biblioteka "Njegoš", Knjaževac.

Question Answering Systems Approaches and Challenges

Reem Alqifari
King Saud University /Riyadh, Saudi Arabia
University of York / York, UK
ralgifary@ksu.edu.sa

Abstract

Question answering (QA) systems permit the user to ask a question using natural language, and the system provides a concise and correct answer. QA systems can be implemented for different types of datasets, structured or unstructured. In this paper, some of the recent studies will be reviewed and the limitations will be discussed. Consequently, the current issues are analyzed with the proposed solutions.

1 Introduction

Question answering (QA), are a type of systems in which a user can ask a question using natural language, and the system provides a concise and correct answer. A QA system is different from a search engine in that the user asks a question and the output is an accurate answer instead of a list of relevant documents. A considerable amount of literature has been published on QA, as it has been an object of research since the 1960s (Green et al., 1961).

There are three paradigms of question answering systems, which are:

- The information retrieval approach or free text QA, in which a question is analyzed to determine the answer type, and then Information Retrieval (IR) methods are performed to search a corpus for an answer (Tan et al. 2015; Feng et al. 2015).

- The knowledge base approach (KB-QA), where the question is reformulated as a predicate that has a semantic representation and the system will search datasets of facts. (Zhang et al. 2016; Hao et al. 2017; Yin et al. 2016).

- Hybrid paradigm, where the system combines free text with a KB. Therefore, the coverage of the system will be wider (the probability to find correct answer will be high)(Das et al., 2017).

Researchers have suggested different measures for evaluating a QA system, including precision and recall. The selection of evaluation metrics is mainly dependent on the QA application or track.

There are many types of questions, but they are generally classified into two types: factoid and non-factoid, also known as complex questions. In factoid questions, the question has a specific answer. In contrast, non-factoid questions are open-ended and may have a variety of possible answers (Cohen and Croft, 2016). Moreover, complex questions compromise multi-relations which means that the reasoning is essential.

Our goal is tackling a standard QA system over KB and free text in addition to a reading comprehension QA. To be specific, we will try to build a system that accurately provides answers for temporal questions. Based on my reading, extracting temporal relations is a challenging process that involves capturing the meaning of temporal prepositions, such as before or during. The main challenge in my research is determining how to overcome the complexity and difficulty of answering complex questions that involve reasoning. Furthermore, we will need to consider the domain dependency issue and the effectiveness of using deep learning approaches. The ultimate objective of this research is to improve the accuracy and efficiency of the state of the art.

2 Related Work

The first attempted question answering system was developed in the 1960s when (Green et al., 1961) built a baseball system, which is a sim-

Proceedings of the Student Research Workshop associated with RANLP-2019, pages 69–75,
Varna, Bulgaria, Sep 2–4, 2019.
https://doi.org/10.26615/issn.2603-2821.2019_011

ple closed domain system that answers a question asked in a natural language using a structured database. This study was followed by different systems with many limitations.

Research began to focus on open-domain questions when the Text REtrieval Conference (TREC) started a QA track in 1999. The TREC annual competition has encouraged many research projects in different languages. There are now some other competitions, such as the SQuAD leaderboard and MS MACRO leaderboard. All of that led to a proliferation of studies in QA.

QA can be applied to closed or open domains. In a closed domain, questions are focused on a particular domain, and the answer is extracted from datasets built for this domain only, such as the insuranceQA dataset (Feng et al., 2015). In contrast, in an open domain, the question can be on any subject, and the QA system uses a large corpus with a variety of topics, such as TREC QA.

There are various research areas and applications for QA, including:

- Standard question answering, where the answer comes from the KB or a free text.

- Dialog systems or chatbots are the system used for chatting with an agent. An example of such a system is Siri.

- Community question answering system, where the user asks or posts a question and receives a variety of answers from other users (community). The system has to validate the answers and choose the most relevant and accurate one.

- Multimedia QA, where the question is about an image or video. So, the system has to be able to capture and understand the features of the image or video.

- Reading comprehension QA (RC-QA), where the system is given a question with a passage, and the answer is selected from that passage.

Each path differs from the other in terms of challenges and problems and may depend on different techniques. However, the number of research is increasing in all applications. That because of the emergence and development of deep learning techniques and availability of datasets. The following sub-sections focus on two tracks that are the scope of the study.

2.1 Question Answering over Knowledge-Bases (KB-QA)

Recently, with the rapid growth of large-scale knowledge bases on the Web, such as DBpedia[1] and Freebase, knowledge bases have become very important resources and promising approaches for open-domain question answering. Three basic approaches are adopted in research into KB-QA (Hao et al., 2017):

- The semantic parsing based (SP-based) approach is focused on constructing a semantic parser that converts a question into structured expressions like logical forms (Yih et al., 2015). Semantic parser is also used to turn natural-language questions into structured queries (SPARQL). It is well known that semantic parser is not a straightforward task.

- The information retrieval or relation extraction (IR-based) approach searches for the answer from the KB based on the question. Ranking is used to select the best answers from the candidate list.

- Deep learning or embedding based: questions and answers are represented using semantic vectors (Hao et al., 2017). Then, a similarity matrix is applied to find the most similar answer. The crucial step is computing the similarity.

The recent methodology has three core stages, mentioned below:

- Topic entity: The goal of this step is to define the main topic of the question. Some researchers have used an API to extract the topic of the questions (Yih et al. 2015; Hao et al. 2017).

- Fact finding: Also known as relation extraction. This used to search for a relation with the defined topic entity, which is mentioned in the question, and then provide candidate knowledge triples. Knowledge completion can be used(Yih et al., 2015).

- Answer selection: This method is used to match the question and candidate triples into semantic vectors, and then calculate the semantic relevance score between them using

---

[1]http://dbpedia.org

the predefined similarity measure. Then, the most similar answer is chosen(Hao et al., 2017).

KB-QA are generally classified into two types: Multi-Relation questions and Single-Relation questions. Multi-Relation questions measure the ability of the system to answer multi-constrained questions. According to (Bao et al., 2016) there are six main constraints. There are three widely used datasets for KB-QA, and all of them are based on the Freebase KB. This means that all of the questions can be answered using Freebase. The SimpleQuestions dataset, introduced by (Hill et al., 2015) named simple because it is tackled the single-relation questions. On the other hand, WebQuestions (Berant et al., 2013) and ComplexQuestions (Bao et al., 2016) are based on multi-relations questions.

Despite the fact that KBs are very large, they are still quite incomplete, missing large percentages of facts. For the QA system, although the answer might not exist in the knowledge base, it can be discovered by using knowledge completion techniques. Some researches have adopted this track to improve the accuracy of QA systems (Toutanova et al., 2016).

The deep learning approach has been widely used in different NLP tasks, including QA. The DL can overcome some limitations, such as the complexity of feature extraction. Also, it can be beneficial for reducing dependency on the rule-based as in the existing SP-based KB-QA systems which affect the generalization. However, the DL methodology has not achieved human performance in QA applications. Hence, Some challenges remain to be tackled, including the lexical gap or vocabulary gap. This means that the user question has a different vocabulary than the KB does. So, the system requires to bridge the gap between the user question and the KB. The problem of the lexical gap can be minimized using word embedding. (Das et al., 2017) tried to overcome the incompleteness and lexical gap by combining text with the KB and using word embedding.

2.2 Reading Comprehension

Reading comprehension (RC) uses questions and answers to test the level of text understanding. Reading comprehension tests are normally used to test the reading level of language learners or children. When RC tests are used to test NL un-derstanding by a computer, this is called machine comprehension. This task requires a machine to answer a question or set of questions from a given passage. The question can be either a multiple-choice or a short-answer question.

RC-QA is challenging, as it involves combination of multiple difficult tasks such as reading, processing, comprehending, reasoning, and finally providing the answer. One of the earliest systems designed to answer reading comprehension tests was QUALM, developed by Lehnert in 1977.

Reading comprehension has gained interest in recent research. There is also a gap between human and machine performance in answering questions because reading comprehension is not about word-based search and context matching. Challenges of machine comprehension QA arise mainly because of reasoning. They include:

- Synthesis: Answering a question requires integrating information distributed across multiple sentences in a passage.

- Paraphrasing: A single sentence in the article may entail or paraphrase the question. Paraphrase recognition may require synonymy and word knowledge.

- Inference: Some answers must be inferred from incomplete information in the passage.

Various deep learning techniques have been applied for reading comprehension. Generally, a variety of models of RNN and attention have been used in recent research such as: (Yu et al. 2018; Xiong et al. 2016; Seo et al. 2016) . Figure 1 reveals the common deep learning architecture that has been used for reading comprehension QA. The main components are:

- Embedding layer: The representation model of the input (the question and the passage), typically Word2Vec or GloVe.

- Encoding layer: The neural network model used for encoding the question and the passage separately. Usually, one of the RNN techniques applied.

- Attention layer: An attention mechanism is applied to capture the relation between the question and the passage.

- Output layer: Generating or finding the answer, depending on the answer type. if the answer is a text span, the output will be the start and the end position of the answer in the passage. A pointer network can be used.

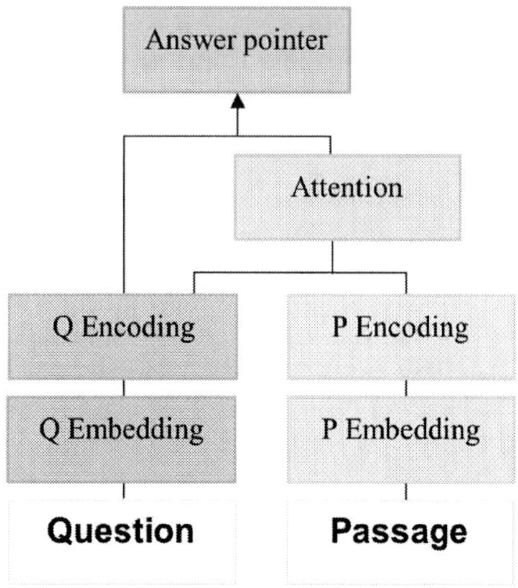

Figure 1: Common Architecture of RC-QA SYSTEM

2.3 Temporal Processing

Temporal language consists of time, event, and temporal relations. Events include occasions, actions, occurrences, and states (Derczynski, 2017). Temporal relations are categorized into three main categories (Pustejovsky et al., 2017):

- Temporal relation (TLINK): Represent the temporal relationship between two events, an event and a time or two times. For example: She submitted the report last week.

- Subordinate (SLINK): Used for modality, evidential and factual. For example: She refused to submit the report.

- Aspectual (ALINK): Only between two events, describing an aspectual connection. For instance: She finished writing the report.

Based on (Bethard et al., 2016), temporal relational extraction is the most difficult step of temporal representation. Temporal QA means the ability to answer any temporal-based question. This encapsulates extracting the temporal information and requires some reasoning. According to (Jia et al., 2018a) and (Bao et al., 2016), the

Temporal question can be classified to four categories:

- Temporal answer, where the question asks about time or date.

- Explicit temporal, in which the question contains an explicit date, time, or event, such as: Who was the king of Saudi Arabia at 2014?

- Implicit temporal, in which the question has no explicit temporal term but contains a term such as before, after, or during.

- Ordinal constraints, in which the rank is needed to answer the question, such as What is the third largest continent?

(Jia et al., 2018a) has indroduced TemQuestions datasets. It has been extracted from three KB-QA datasets (Free917, WebQuestions, and ComplexQuestions), whose answer sets are based on Freebase. The released of this datasets has been followed by an implementation of Temporal QA system called TEQUILA by (Jia et al., 2018b). The main limitation of TEQUILA is that it is based on the rule-based approach.

3 Problem Statement and Proposed Contribution

Different types of temporal-based questions of various levels of complexity can be tackled. Temporal reasoning is challenging, and complicated because some events are vague. Also, extracting the temporal relations, which is essential step to answer a temporal question, is challenging. A brief summarization of the recent studies in different directions of KB-QA are provided in Table 1.

As previously mentioned in this paper, the extraction of temporal relations has not yet been solved. Temporal questions can found in KB-QA and RC-QA. Therefore, both tracks might be addressed and different issues might be considered. For example, as mentioned previously, KB-QA has many challenges including: lexical gap, scalability and complexity of understanding natural language questions. On the other hand, the main issue with the RC-QA is understanding the text and reasoning over multiple sentences.

3.1 Research Questions

Based on the explanation above, we must consider the following research questions:

Dataset	State of the art	Evaluation metrics	Methodology	Limitations
WebQuestions	(Yih et al., 2015)	F1=52.5%	SP-based..CNN for semantic similarity	Handcrafted features
WebQuestions	(Hao et al., 2017)	F1=42.9%	IR-based.. Bi-LSTM with cross attention model	
TempQuestions	(Jia et al., 2018b)	F1=36.7%	SP-based..	Hand-coded query templates

Table 1: Summarize some of the recent work on KB-QA.

- What methods can alleviate the out-of-vocabulary problem? How to bridge the lexical gap between the vocabulary of the natural language question and the KB or the context lexical?

- How to understand and model the semantic feature of the complex questions? What is the best method: Is it the semantic parsing or decomposition using reinforcement learning? How to minimize the reliance on the hand-coded rules?

- How to handle the reasoning over the complex questions. And what is the most efficient memory and attention mechanism that should be considered?

- How to represent the temporal questions without using the pre-defiend list of expressions that has been used in (Yih et al., 2015) and in and (Bao et al., 2016)?

3.2 Potential Contribution

Neural turing machines (NTMs) (Graves et al., 2014) together with reinforcement learning (RL) is expected to provide new mechanisms for handling long-term memory that is vital for QA. Hence, the application of NTMs and reinforcement learning for QA and RC will be studied. Using NTM in some problem such as question answering can improve the system because it can mimic the human memory. As NTM can save the information that is useful for answering the question. Although LSTM has internal memory stored in its hidden states, NTM has external memory. Hence, the system can have unlimited memory, and that effectively extended the capabilities of NN. Therefore, using NTM is promising for solving QA problems as QA systems require large and persistent memory. Moreover, considering the difficulty of temporal reasoning, a temporal linkage can be added to the NTM which is an inspiration from the DNC (Graves et al., 2016). Also, applying RL either for query graph generation or for the question decomposition is promising.

In order to overcome the out-of-vocabulary issue as well as the lexical gap, three main strategies will be applied: firstly, using character embedding for the question to overcome the misspelled word or typos. Secondly, using pre-trained word embedding for the question and the context. Also, combine the context with global knowledge, such as Wikipedia or commonsense knowledge.

The proposed approaches will be applied to different datasets (KB and RC) such as WebQuestions and MS MARCO or SQuAD. Additionally, answering temporal questions will be tackled.

4 Conclusion and Future Direction

Despite the promising results of applying deep learning for QA, there are some issued that need to be tackled. Therefore, we will try to handle some of the limitations. This encapsulate understanding of the complex questions, reasoning, and lexical gap. The importance and originality of this study are that it will explore the application of NTMs and reinforcement learning for the complex and temporal questions in KB-QA and RC-QA. Research questions that could be asked include whether one architecture can be applied for both KB-QA and RC-QA and provide high accuracy. Most research studies have considered them as two different problems, but they might not be, as the input text in RC can be seen as a KB.

Acknowledgments

I would like to thank my research supervisors, Dr. Suresh Manandhar, and Prof. Hend Al-Khalifa.Without their support and advice, this paper would have never been accomplished.

References

Junwei Bao, Nan Duan, Zhao Yan, Ming Zhou, and Tiejun Zhao. 2016. Constraint-Based Question Answering with Knowledge Graph. *Proceedings of COLING 2016, the 26th International Conference on Computational Linguistics: Technical Papers* pages 2503–2514. https://aclanthology.info/papers/C16-1236/c16-1236.

Jonathan Berant, Andrew Chou, Roy Frostig, and Percy Liang. 2013. Semantic Parsing on Freebase from Question-Answer Pairs. In *Proceedings of the 2013 Conference on Empirical Methods in Natural Language Processing*. Association for Computational Linguistics, Seattle, Washington, USA, pages 1533–1544. http://www.aclweb.org/anthology/D13-1160.

Steven Bethard, Guergana Savova, Wei-Te Chen, Leon Derczynski, James Pustejovsky, and Marc Verhagen. 2016. Semeval-2016 task 12: Clinical tempeval. In *Proceedings of the 10th International Workshop on Semantic Evaluation (SemEval-2016)*. pages 1052–1062.

Daniel Cohen and W. Bruce Croft. 2016. End to End Long Short Term Memory Networks for Non-Factoid Question Answering. In *Proceedings of the 2016 ACM International Conference on the Theory of Information Retrieval*. ACM, New York, NY, USA, ICTIR '16, pages 143–146. https://doi.org/10.1145/2970398.2970438.

Rajarshi Das, Manzil Zaheer, Siva Reddy, and Andrew McCallum. 2017. Question Answering on Knowledge Bases and Text using Universal Schema and Memory Networks. *arXiv:1704.08384 [cs]* ArXiv: 1704.08384. http://arxiv.org/abs/1704.08384.

Leon R.A. Derczynski. 2017. *Automatically Ordering Events and Times in Text*, volume 677 of *Studies in Computational Intelligence*. Springer International Publishing, Cham. https://doi.org/10.1007/978-3-319-47241-6.

Minwei Feng, Bing Xiang, Michael R. Glass, Lidan Wang, and Bowen Zhou. 2015. Applying Deep Learning to Answer Selection: A Study and An Open Task. *arXiv:1508.01585 [cs]* ArXiv: 1508.01585. http://arxiv.org/abs/1508.01585.

Alex Graves, Greg Wayne, and Ivo Danihelka. 2014. Neural Turing Machines. *arXiv:1410.5401 [cs]* ArXiv: 1410.5401. http://arxiv.org/abs/1410.5401.

Alex Graves, Greg Wayne, Malcolm Reynolds, Tim Harley, Ivo Danihelka, Agnieszka Grabska-Barwińska, Sergio Gómez Colmenarejo, Edward Grefenstette, Tiago Ramalho, John Agapiou, et al. 2016. Hybrid computing using a neural network with dynamic external memory. *Nature* 538(7626):471.

Jr. Bert F. Green, Alice K. Wolf, Carol Chomsky, and Kenneth Laughery. 1961. Baseball: An Automatic Question-answerer. In *Papers Presented at the May 9-11, 1961, Western Joint IRE-AIEE-ACM Computer Conference*. ACM, New York, NY, USA, IRE-AIEE-ACM '61 (Western), pages 219–224. https://doi.org/10.1145/1460690.1460714.

Yanchao Hao, Yuanzhe Zhang, Kang Liu, Shizhu He, Zhanyi Liu, Hua Wu, and Jun Zhao. 2017. An End-to-End Model for Question Answering over Knowledge Base with Cross-Attention Combining Global Knowledge. In *ACL*. https://doi.org/10.18653/v1/P17-1021.

Felix Hill, Antoine Bordes, Sumit Chopra, and Jason Weston. 2015. The Goldilocks Principle: Reading Children's Books with Explicit Memory Representations. *arXiv:1511.02301 [cs]* ArXiv: 1511.02301. http://arxiv.org/abs/1511.02301.

Zhen Jia, Abdalghani Abujabal, Rishiraj Saha Roy, Jannik Strötgen, and Gerhard Weikum. 2018a. Tempquestions: A benchmark for temporal question answering. In *Companion Proceedings of the The Web Conference 2018*. International World Wide Web Conferences Steering Committee, Republic and Canton of Geneva, Switzerland, WWW '18, pages 1057–1062. https://doi.org/10.1145/3184558.3191536.

Zhen Jia, Abdalghani Abujabal, Rishiraj Saha Roy, Jannik Strötgen, and Gerhard Weikum. 2018b. Tequila: Temporal question answering over knowledge bases. In *Proceedings of the 27th ACM International Conference on Information and Knowledge Management*. ACM, New York, NY, USA, CIKM '18, pages 1807–1810. https://doi.org/10.1145/3269206.3269247.

James Pustejovsky, Harry Bunt, and Annie Zaenen. 2017. Designing Annotation Schemes: From Theory to Model. In Nancy Ide and James Pustejovsky, editors, *Handbook of Linguistic Annotation*, Springer Netherlands, Dordrecht, pages 21–72. https://doi.org/10.1007/978-94-024-0881-2-2.

Min Joon Seo, Aniruddha Kembhavi, Ali Farhadi, and Hannaneh Hajishirzi. 2016. Bidirectional attention flow for machine comprehension. *ArXiv* abs/1611.01603.

Ming Tan, Cicero dos Santos, Bing Xiang, and Bowen Zhou. 2015. LSTM-based Deep Learning Models for Non-factoid Answer Selection https://arxiv.org/abs/1511.04108.

Kristina Toutanova, Xi Victoria Lin, Scott Wen-tau Yih, Hoifung Poon, and Chris Quirk. 2016. Compositional Learning of Embeddings for Relation Paths in Knowledge Bases and Text. *Microsoft Research* https://www.microsoft.com/en-us/research/publication/compositional-learning-of-embeddings-for-relation-paths-in-knowledge-bases-and-text/.

Caiming Xiong, Stephen Merity, and Richard Socher. 2016. Dynamic Memory Networks for Visual and Textual Question Answering. In *Proceedings of the 33rd International Conference on International Conference on Machine Learning - Volume 48*. JMLR.org, New York, NY, USA, ICML'16, pages 2397–2406. http://dl.acm.org/citation.cfm?id=3045390.3045643.

Wen-tau Yih, Ming-Wei Chang, Xiaodong He, and
Jianfeng Gao. 2015. Semantic Parsing via Staged
Query Graph Generation: Question Answering with
Knowledge Base. In *Proceedings of the 53rd
Annual Meeting of the Association for Computa-
tional Linguistics and the 7th International Joint
Conference on Natural Language Processing (Vol-
ume 1: Long Papers)*. Association for Compu-
tational Linguistics, Beijing, China, pages 1321–
1331. https://doi.org/10.3115/v1/P15-1128.

Wenpeng Yin, Mo Yu, Bing Xiang, Bowen Zhou,
and Hinrich SchACEtze. 2016. Simple Question
Answering by Attentive Convolutional Neural Network. *arXiv:1606.03391 [cs]* ArXiv: 1606.03391.
http://arxiv.org/abs/1606.03391.

Adams Wei Yu, David Dohan, Minh-Thang Luong, Rui
Zhao, Kai Chen, Mohammad Norouzi, and Quoc V
Le. 2018. QANET: COMBINING LOCAL CON-
VOLUTION WITH GLOBAL SELF-ATTENTION
FOR READING COMPRE- HENSION. page 16.

Yuanzhe Zhang, Kang Liu, Shizhu He, Guoliang Ji,
Zhanyi Liu, Hua Wu, and Jun Zhao. 2016. Question Answering over Knowledge Base with Neural
Attention Combining Global Knowledge Information. *arXiv:1606.00979 [cs]* ArXiv: 1606.00979.
http://arxiv.org/abs/1606.00979.

Adding Linguistic Knowledge to NLP Tasks for Bulgarian: The Verb Paradigm Patterns

Ivaylo Radev

LMaKP

IICT-BAS

Sofia, Bulgaria

radev@bultreebank.org

Abstract

The paper reports pn a work on constructing automatically analytical paradigm of Bulgarian verbs on the bases of several existing language resources like Bulgarian inflection lexicon, Bulgarian Valency lexicons, BulTreeBank Bulgarian WordNet. The paper also discusses some possible usages of this new lexical resource containing Bulgarian verb paradigms and their English translations. This type of data can be used for machine translation, generation of pseudo corpora/language exercises, evaluation of parsers, and other tasks.

1 Introduction

The lack of training resources is a constant problem for many tasks within NLP. This is particularly true for languages like Bulgarian that are less resourced in some aspects. Automatically created labeled datasets are often seen as a solution to this problem. The creation of such data usually follows some kind of bootstrapping where the procedure starts with a set of seed elements and then an algorithm selects similar examples from a large corpus. Following this schema, the process could start with training a system on a small existing dataset and then analyze a large corpus from which new examples are to be selected; see for example (Mihalcea, 2002). Another strategy to produce automatically annotated data is to build pseudo corpora from existing resources; this is the approach applied for the creation of semantically annotated corpora from WordNets via Random Walk on Graphs algorithms (Goikoetxea et al., 2015). The algorithm for random walk on the knowledge graph of WordNet traverses the graph and emits a lemma and/or a word sense for each node respectively.

In our work, we produce syntactically correct sentences on the basis of several integrated resources for Bulgarian, including an inflectional lexicon, WordNet, a valency lexicon and a set of patterns for constructing the whole paradigms of Bulgarian verbs and the corresponding simple Subject + Verb + Indirect Object + Direct Object sentences exhausting all the possible word order alternations. In this paper, we demonstrate the patterns and the ways they can be used.

The Bulgarian verb is the grammatically richest part of speech (POS) of the language. The number of its synthetic forms goes up to 52. The analytical part of the verbal paradigm is much larger and comprises more than a thousand forms. Here we extend the paradigm to include not only verbal forms *per se* (simple forms, participles, auxiliary verbs and the particles да and ще) but also personal pronoun clitics for direct and indirect objects. Thus, for each verb we construct thousands of patterns which represent unique verbal forms. For example, a personal transitive verb like чета ("read") in present tense, 1st person, singular can be accompanied by one or, in this case, two clitics to form the following sentence:

(1)   Чета им   я .
        Read-I them.DAT her .

        Аз им   я чета .
        I   them.DAT her read .

        'I am reading it to them.'

One important characteristic of Bulgarian verbal forms is that they are in fact full-fledged simple sentences in their finite forms. Bulgarian is a pro-drop language and in most cases the direct and indirect objects can be optional as well. There are, of course, some exceptions to the rule. For example, the verb състоя се ("consist of") takes an obligatory indirect object. We rely on a valency lexicon of Bulgarian for presenting the selectional

Proceedings of the Student Research Workshop associated with RANLP-2019, pages 76–82,
Varna, Bulgaria, Sep 2–4, 2019.
https://doi.org/10.26615/issn.2603-2821.2019_012

restrictions of such cases. To sum up, we can generate thousands of simple sentences automatically, which in turn will benefit the creation of a lot of other resources. Even by itself, the dataset is valuable enough since it will contain patterns with up to 10253 verb paradigm members, including verbal complexes with all the possible combinations of subject, direct, and indirect object clitics, negative (няма, не), and interrogative particles (ли).

The paper is structured as follows: the next section discusses related work. Section 3 presents the extended verb paradigm (patterns sets). Section 4 surveys the possible impact of the paradigm data on NLP tasks. Section 5 concludes the paper and outlines future work.

2 Related Work

Previous efforts on adding linguistic knowledge to statistical machine translation for Bulgarian were done in (Simov et al., 2015). The paper reports on experiments done with machine translation from Bulgarian-to-English and English-to-Bulgarian under the project QTLeap.

The authors report problems with the so-called out-of-training word forms, word form pairs that do not appear in the parallel corpora used for the training. In order to solve this problem a parallel Bulgarian-English morphological lexicon was added to the parallel corpora. This lexicon was used in the POS tagging step, to provide all the possible tags for the known words and, in the lemmatization step, to convert each word form into its lemma.

The lexicon of 70 000 aligned word forms was constructed by exploiting several preexisting resources. First, word form lexicons for both languages were mapped to the corresponding part of the bilingual lexicon. Then, the corresponding word forms were aligned on the basis of morphological features like number, degree, definiteness, etc. This linguistic knowledge has been added gradually as factors in the MOSES system.

The paper reports a positive impact of the aligned word form parallel lexicon on the translation in both directions, but the addition of the definite forms for English did not change the result.

The lexical resource WordNet (WN) has established itself as one of the most used and popular language data resources in the field of NLP. WN can be described as a kind of thesaurus that groups word meanings or senses together and labels the semantic relations among them.

The BulTreeBank Bulgarian WordNet (BTB-WN) — (Simov et al., 2019) is a newly created and expanding lexical resource for Bulgarian language. It currently contains 22 000 synsets manually mapped to the Princeton WordNet (PWN) and continues to grow due to the process of linking it with the Bulgarian Wikipedia. The role of the BTB-WN is to provide lexical and semantic data for NLP tasks for Bulgarian such as sense disambiguation (WSD), relation extraction, named entity and multiword expression (MWE) parsing, machine translation, etc.

One example for experimentation with WN is (Mihalcea, 2002). The paper describes an algorithm for the automatic generation of GenCor, a large sense tagged corpora, for participation in SENSEVAL-2. The generation algorithm works in three steps: (1) creation of a set of seeds (sense tagged examples from SemCor; WN and rule creation); (2) searching in the Web with the seed expressions; (3) disambiguation of words in a small text snippet surrounding the seed expressions.

The idea of creating sense tagged examples out of WordNet is based on the assumption that each example and its corresponding synset are properly linked, which allows to assign the correct sense to at least one word in the examples. The relations between words taken into consideration are identity, synonymy, hypernymy, hyponymy, and sibling terms.

The usage of WN in recent years and efforts to link it with other resources (BabelNet; UBY) show that it is beneficial to use multiple language resources at once, especially for low-resource languages that do not have such resources or their existing resources are small in size.

Another grammatical data resource used in NLP tasks for Bulgarian is the valence lexicon presented as part of the Bulgarian Ontology-based Lexicon (Osenova et al., 2012). The lexicon exploits the relation between ontology and text. This lexicon is mapped to an ontology in order to connect lexical units to their conceptual meanings. Additionally, the lexicon contains phonological, morphological, and syntactic linguistic knowledge.

A related paper (Osenova and Simov, 2015) reports that the lexicon contains 4113 valency frames coupled with the respective meanings and that it covers 1903 lemmas. It considers the verbs as the most important part of speech for the task of semantic role annotation.

The valency frames are extracted from the Bul-TreeBank, manually linked with verb senses and detailed participants with respect to the usage, and then returned back into the treebank (Osenova et al., 2012). This ensures that the sense and the frame are appropriate for the respective usage for each verb occurrence in the treebank. The semantic classes of the verbs are transferred by the mappings of the Bulgarian valency lexicon to the PWN, which, together with the valency frames, helps in the process of selection of the appropriate semantic roles. After that the semantic roles are transferred to the corresponding constituents in the tree of the verb occurrence.

3   The Verbal Paradigm Patterns

In this section we present the types of patterns which are used for the generation of all members of the extended verbal paradigm. In order to generate all of these forms we create patterns that include the verb synthetic form, clitics, auxiliaries, etc.

From all the parts of speech in Bulgarian, the verb bears the most information. It contains grammatical information not only about the predicate expressing an event, but also for the participants in this event. The grammatical characteristics of the verb are: 9 tenses (1 present tense, 4 past tenses and 4 future tenses); perfective and imperfective aspect; singular and plural number; first, second and third person; gender in the participle forms; active and passive voice (although some argue for one more — reflexive); indicative, imperative, conditional mood, and three evidentials: renarrative, dubitative, and conclusive. Thus the patterns represent the allowed combinations of these forms and features. Each pattern for a given form consists of a form of the main verb and some auxiliary elements which include auxiliary verbs as well as some verbal particles. Because we want to express also the negative, interrogative, and passive voice forms, we include such forms in the verbal paradigm patterns. The last element of the extended verbal paradigm is the valency potential of the verb. Here we assume only the internal arguments of the verb — the subject, the direct object, and the indirect object. All of them could be represented via nominative, accusative or dative clitics.

These clitics can be in singular or plural number, and in first, second, or third person. Additionally, we create a pattern for each possible word order of the corresponding main verb form, auxiliary, verbal particles and clitics. In our work we consider a verb form to be determined by its grammatical characteristics. Its realization based on omitted pronouns (clitics) or movement in the word ordering of the particles and pronouns is called variation.

All this results in many forms and variations. The extended paradigm of the verb чета ("read") contains 1205 verb forms and 10253 variations with explicit subject, direct, and indirect object clitics.

The initial idea behind the construction of a Bulgarian verb paradigm pattern set was for it to be used in the improvement of the coverage of the Bulgarian treebank. The motivation for this is that only a small percentage of the verb forms could be found in the available corpora of Bulgarian. For example, the form Някой чете нещо "Someone reads something" is basically omnipresent and the form Щял съм бил да им я чета "(they doubt) I would be reading it to them" is very rarely attested in everyday (web) language. We have created verb paradigm pattern sets for nine types of Bulgarian verbs — see Table 1. These types of verbs are described by the grammatical features of their stems and the number of the paradigm members vary for each type of verb.

The representative verbs for each type were selected randomly to cover basic grammatical information for: personal/impersonal verbs; transitive/intransitive verbs; reflexive verbs and the perfect/progressive aspect of verbs. All of the paradigm patterns are encoded manually for the representative verb of the corresponding type. Additionally, each lexical item in each pattern receives its POS tag from the BulTreeBank tagset — (Simov et al., 2004). Also, the lexical items in the patterns are trivially lemmatized.

As it was mentioned, each of these lemmas is conjugated in all possible verb forms for tense, person, number, mood and voice. The clitics for subject, direct and indirect object are added. The forms also include tree more variations: negation, question and a combination of the two. In some cases more than one word ordering are possible. The negation variants are formed with the particle не "not". For example:

No	Verb	Features	Transcription	Translation
1	може	impers; intr; ipfv; mod	'mozhe'	can
2	трябва	impers; intr; ipfv; mod	'tryabva'	have to
3	вървя	pers; intr; ipfv	'varvya'	I walk
4	чета	pers; tr; ipfv	'cheta'	I read
5	прочета	pers; tr; pfv	'procheta'	I read (it all)
6	сърби ме	pers; intr; ipfv; acc	'sarbi me'	It is iching me
7	домъчнява ми	impers; intr; ipfv; dat	'domachnyava mi'	(I) start to feel grief (for something)
8	смея се	pers; intr; ipfv; refl	'smeya se'	I am laughing
9	изсмея се	pers; intr; ipfv; refl	'izsmeya se'	I am laughing (once)

Table 1: The current verbs in the paradigm resource. Grammatical features: impers = impersonal, pers = personal, tr = transitive, intr = intransitive, pfv = perfective, imperfective = ipfv, refl = reflexive, mod = modal, dat = dative clitic verb, acc = accusative clitic verb.

(2) Не им   я чета .
     Not them.DAT her read-I .

     'I am not reading it to them.'

The interrogative variants are formed with the interrogative particle ли. For example:

(3) Чета ли   им   я   ?
     Read-I INTER them.DAT her ?

     'Am I reading it to them?'

Finally, the combination of negative and interrogative variants has some possible word orders:

(4) Не им   я   чета ли   ?
     Not them.DAT her read-I INTER ?

     Не им   ли   я   чета ?
     Not them.DAT INTER her read-I ?

     'Am I not reading it to them?'

As was mentioned above, each of the variations is also a plausible simple sentence in Bulgarian. There are a few exceptions like participles that can be used only in attributive constructions and gerunds.

Finally, possible translations to English are included after every form. It is important to note that the two Bulgarian aspects are considered different lemmas and the Bulgarian language does not use continuous tenses as the English does. A present continuous tense does not exist in Bulgarian. Both languages have imperfect tenses, but only in name. In Bulgarian, the perfective and imperfective aspects have forms for imperfect tense. These dissimilarities lead to variations in the translations of the tenses. The translation patterns depend only on the forms of the main verb and its translation into English.

Up to here we have presented the construction of verb paradigm pattern sets for the nine main types of Bulgarian verbs. In order to apply them to arbitrary verbs we need to link the patterns with other language resources. More precisely to an inflectional lexicon, a valency lexicon and a Bulgarian WordNet. Each of these resources provides pieces of the puzzle that are necessary for the application of the patterns.

The first step is to determine the paradigm types via mapping the paradigm pattern type to the verb type. Data for the verb types will come from the inflectional morphological lexicon. On the basis of the grammatical features we select the correct verb pattern set. For example the lemma of the verb дарявам ("to gift") has the same POS tag as the verb чета ("read") and is also transitive and imperfective. Thus from the inflectional lexicon we receive the synthetic paradigm of the verb and its grammatical features of the stem.

The next step is to extract information about the possible clitics of the verb. This information is available within the Bulgarian valency lexicon. From the pattern set and the POS tags we know that чета ("read") has dative and accusative clitic. Then we need to check the frame for дарявам ("to gift") if it can also have direct and indirect object to transform the pattern:

(5) Чета ли   им   я   ?
     Read-I INTER them.DAT her ?

(6) Дарявам ли   им   я   ?
     Gift-I   INTER them.DAT her ?

The last necessary bit of information is the English translation, which we find within the BTB-WN. As was presented above, the valency lexicon was integrated with BTB-WN. Thus, when we select a Bulgarian verb together with its inflectional type and valency frame we also determine its potential senses within BTB-WN. The mapping from BTB-WN to the English WordNet is used to select the English verb.

Utilizing all this information, we could construct the whole extended paradigm of the selected verb and the corresponding translations in English:

(7) Чета ли   им   я ?
     Read-I INTER them.DAT her ?

     'Am I reading it to them?'

(8) Дарявам ли   им   я ?
     Gift-I   INTER them.DAT her ?

     'Am I gifting it to them?'

4 Application of the Extended Verbal Paradigm

In this section we present some applications of the generated extended verbal paradigms. Some of these applications require extensions of the patterns in order to add the necessary linguistic knowledge to the verbal forms.

The immediate NLP applications of the new language resource include POS tagging and lemmatization. Although we have the rules by which the verbal forms are generated and we could easily turn them into an analytical module, the resource could be used for training and testing statistical or neural network POS taggers. Because most of the clitics and many of the verbs are ambiguous, the task of POS tagging is not trivial.

Another obvious application is in the area of statistical and neural network machine translation, similarly to the experiments reported in (Simov et al., 2015). We hope that in this way the MT system would be able to learn to translate analytical verbal forms.

In order to support other NLP tasks we need to extend the resource with more linguistic knowledge. To support dependency parsing we need to convert each verbal form which represents a sentence into Universal Dependency (UD) format. This is straightforwardly done via rules for each of auxiliaries, clitics and particles. For example the sentence from above:

(9) Аз им   я   чета .
     I   them.DAT her read .

     'I am reading it to them.'

is converted to the following UD tree depicted in Figure 1 for the example 9.

After converting the extended paradigms into UD trees provides an useful resource for training and testing UD parsers. But it is obvious that the utilities of simple sentences comprising a verb, auxiliaries, particles and clitics is not huge. In order to make them really useful we need to include also full-fledged arguments. In order to do this we need to extended the patterns with positions of the full-fledged arguments with respect to the other components of the verbal forms.

Then using the mapping from the main verb to the valency lexicon we could determine the sense annotation of the arguments of the verb. These senses are linked to appropriate synsets in BTB-WN. This allows to select appropriate lemmas for each argument. Then having grammatical features for each argument stated in the verbal form we could generate the correct word form for the arguments.

If for the verb чета we have the notion that an "agent" can read an "information object", we can substitute the pronouns with full words. In this way we convert the sentence:

(10) Той им   я   чете .
      He them.DAT her read .

      'He is reading it to them'

into the sentence:

(11) Учителят чете книга на учениците .
      Teacher-the read book to students-the .

      'The teacher is reading book to the students.'

Another kind of data that can be imported from WN comes from its "instance-of" relation for generating sentences with named entities:

(12) Барак Обама чете Властелинът на
      Barack Obama read lord-the   of
      пръстените на учениците .
      rings-the   to students-the .

      'Barack Obama is reading the Lord of the rings to the students.'

We can also use the mapping of BTB-WN to PWN to translate the positions in the pseudo sentences bidirectionally from Bulgarian to English and from English to Bulgarian. This will be an even better source of parallel data for machine translation models.

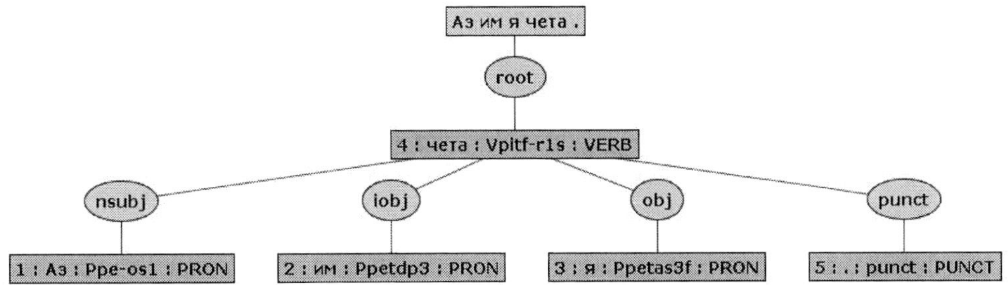

Figure 1: UD tree for the example 9.

It is also easy to extend the conversion module in order to represent such sentences into UD format. The other consequence of the procedure for the generation of sentences is that we know the senses of each word in them. In this way the new sentences could be used for training and testing UD parsers and modules for the Word Sense Disambiguation task.

The Bulgarian language (as a Balkan one) also uses clitic doubling:

(13) Учителят им   я   чете книгата на
      Teacher-the them.DAT her read book-the to
      учениците .
      students-the .

      'The teacher is reading a book to the students.'

This phenomenon is rarely seen in corpora, but it is used in everyday communication. It allows for logical emphasis and relates contrast. In cases where the head of the object is in front of the predicate the doubling is mandatory. It may be used for both direct and indirect objects.

The good thing about this kind of transformations is that the information for each position in the string is known in advance and everything generated by the automatic system using these resources will have a morpho-tag, lemma, UD annotation, sense disambiguation and translation to English. Another benefit is the control over the parameters for generation; the process can be tuned to get data for specific task.

Corpora containing data from news media, web crawlers and social networks often do not cover all of the linguistic knowledge for a given language. We need pseudo corpora that add this missing information for the training and evaluation of natural language parsers. This kind of pseudo corpora can be generated automatically. The automated method for the generation of training and evaluation data is a core one in the field of NLP and it has been in use for many years.

A resource consisting of sentence strings that combine morphological information, verb frames and sense annotation can be used as the basis for rule-based generation of Universal Dependencies trees. The combination of word sense and verb will provide data for restricting the agents and the positions for direct and indirect objects. This can be done first for Bulgarian and later for English.

5 Conclusion and Future Work

In this paper we present the construction of extended verbal paradigms. The integration of these resources with other language resources like a valency lexicon, BTB-WN and a morphological lexicon converts these paradigms into a well annotated corpus of simple sentences. Thus, the verb paradigm patterns show promise for positive impact on various NLP tasks. The future work on linking it to other linguistic data resources will allow for more specific experiments to be conducted.

One criticism of the approach for constructing full-fledged sentences is that the selected full-fledged subjects, direct and indirect objects are retrieved from WordNet quite randomly. In this way the resulting sentences are far from natural ones. In order to address this problem, in the future we envisage to extract examples of co-occurrences of subjects and objects from automatically parsed corpora and to experiment with the extracted phrases to generate new sentences.

Another task is to experiment with reverse parsing. For instance, taking one sample sentence from real text corpora and transforming it into a new sentence with a rarer verb form. We expect to be able to convert sentences like this one:

(14) Учителят им   чете книга .
      Teacher-the them.DAT read book   .

      'The teacher is reading a book to them.'

to sentences like this one:

(15) Бил ли   им   е чел
      was INTER them.DAT is read.PTCP.SG.M
      учителят книга ?
      teacher-the book   ?

      'Has the teacher read a book to them?'

Our next task will be to evaluate experimentally the usefulness of this new resource. We plan to perform experiments for each of the tasks: POS tagging, UD parsing and WSD.

Acknowledgments

This work was partially supported by the *Bulgarian Ministry of Education and Science under the National Research Programme "Young scientists and postdoctoral students" approved by DCM # 577 / 17.08.2018* and by *the Bulgarian National Interdisciplinary Research e-Infrastructure for Resources and Technologies in favor of the Bulgarian Language and Cultural Heritage, part of the EU infrastructures CLARIN and DARIAH – CLaDA-BG*, Grant number DO01-164/28.08.2018.

References

Josu Goikoetxea, Aitor Soroa, and Eneko Agirre. 2015. Random walks and neural network language models on knowledge bases. In *HLT-NAACL*, pages 1434–1439. The Association for Computational Linguistics.

Rada F. Mihalcea. 2002. Bootstrapping large sense tagged corpora. In *Proceedings of the Third International Conference on Language Resources and Evaluation (LREC'02)*, Las Palmas, Canary Islands - Spain. European Language Resources Association (ELRA).

Petya Osenova and Kiril Simov. 2015. Semantic role annotation in bultreebank. In *Proceedings of the Fourteenth International Workshop on Treebanks and Linguistic Theories (TLT14)*, pages 148–156, Warsaw, Poland. TLT14 2015.

Petya Osenova, Kiril Simov, Laska Laskova, and Stanislava Kancheva. 2012. A treebank-driven creation of an ontovalence verb lexicon for Bulgarian. In *Proceedings of the Eight International Conference on Language Resources and Evaluation (LREC'12)*, pages 2636–2640, Istanbul, Turkey. LREC 2012.

Kiril Simov, Petya Osenova, Laska Laskova, Ivajlo Radev, and Zara Kancheva. 2019. Aligning the Bulgarian BTB WordNet with the Bulgarian Wikipedia. In *Proceedings of the 10th Global WordNet Conference*.

Kiril Simov, Petya Osenova, and Milena Slavcheva. 2004. BTB-TR03: BulTreeBank Morphosyntactic Tagset. Technical report, Bulgarian Academy of Sciences.

Kiril Simov, Iliana Simova, Velislava Todorova, and Petya Osenova. 2015. Factored models for deep machine translation. In *Proceedings of the 1st Deep Machine Translation Workshop (DMTW 2015)*, pages 97–105.

Multilingual Complex Word Identification: Convolutional Neural Networks with Morphological and Linguistic Features

Kim Cheng Sheang
LaSTUS / TALN / DTIC
Universitat Pompeu Fabra
Barcelona, Spain
`kimcheng.sheang@upf.edu`

Abstract

Complex Word Identification (CWI) is an essential task in helping Lexical Simplification (LS) identify the difficult words that should be simplified. In this paper, we present an approach to CWI based on Convolutional Neural Networks (CNN) trained on pre-trained word embeddings with morphological and linguistic features. Generally, the majority of works on CWI are either feature-engineered or neural network with word embeddings. Both approaches have advantages and limitations, so here we combine both approaches in order to achieve higher performance and still support multilingualism. Our evaluation has shown that our system achieves quite similar performance as the state-of-the-art system for English, and it outperforms the state-of-the-art systems for both Spanish and German.

1   Introduction

Text Simplification (TS) (Saggion, 2017) is a research field which aims at developing solutions to transform texts into simpler paraphrases. Generally, there are two types of TS: Lexical Simplification (lexical-level simplification) and Syntactic Simplification (sentence-level simplification).

The research on TS has become more attractive in recent years because of its benefits as a tool for reading aids or help improve the performance of other Natural Language Processing (NLP) tasks. TS has been shown useful for developing reading aids for children (Siddharthan, 2002; Watanabe et al., 2009), non-native speakers (Siddharthan, 2002), people with intellectual disabilities (Bott et al., 2012; Saggion et al., 2015). Moreover, TS can also be used as a preprocess-ing step to improve results of many NLP tasks, e.g., Parsing (Chandrasekar et al., 1996), Information Extraction (Evans, 2011; Jonnalagadda and Gonzalez, 2010), Question Generation (Bernhard et al., 2012), Text Summarization (Siddharthan et al., 2004), and Machine Translation (Štajner and Popovic, 2016).

Lexical Simplification (LS) simplifies text mainly by substituting difficult and less frequently-used words with simpler equivalents. Typically, the pipeline of LS comprises the following steps: complex word identification, substitution generation, substitution selection, and substitution ranking (Paetzold and Specia, 2015).

In this work we concentrate on Complex Word Identification (CWI), a core component of LS, which is used to identify difficult words or phrases that are needed to be simplified. Language difficulty often comes at the lexical level, so simply applying the LS alone could help improve reader understanding and information retention (Leroy et al., 2013).

In this paper, we describe our work on CWI based on deep learning approach called Convolutional Neural Networks (CNN) in combination with word embeddings and engineered-features. The task is to create a model that learns from examples and then uses it to classify any target text in a given sentence as complex or non-complex. As it will be shown, our approach achieves state of the art performance in Spanish and German data, and almost state of the art performance in English data.

We carry out our experiments on data from the Complex Word Identification Shared Task 2018 (Yimam et al., 2017b). Here are two examples from the English and Spanish datasets:

En: Both China and the Philippines **flexed their muscles** on Wednesday.

Proceedings of the Student Research Workshop associated with RANLP-2019, pages 83–89,
Varna, Bulgaria, Sep 2–4, 2019.
https://doi.org/10.26615/issn.2603-2821.2019_013

Es: Allston es un **vecindario** (munici-pio) de Boston, en los Estados Unidos, ubicado en la parte occidental de la ciu-dad.

The target text **flexed their muscles** in the English sentence and **vecindario** in the Spanish sentence are annotated as complex by at least one annotator.

In Section 2, we give an overview of recent research on CWI. Section 3, we describe all the details about the implementation of our system. Section 4 is about the details of the datasets we use in the experiments. Section 5, we present the performance of our system with some discussion. Finally, Section 6 is our conclusion and future work.

2   Related Work

There are many different techniques have been introduced so far to identify complex words (Paetzold and Specia, 2016b; Yimam et al., 2018). It is obvious that feature-based approaches remain the best, but deep learning approaches have become more popular and achieved impressive results.

Gooding and Kochmar (2018) proposed a feature-based approach for monolingual English datasets. The system used lexical features such as number of characters, number of syllables, number of synonyms, word n-gram, POS tags, dependency parse relations, number of words grammatically related to the target word, and Google n-gram word frequencies. It also used psycholinguistic features such as word familiarity rating, number of phonemes, imageability rating, concreteness rating, number of categories, samples, written frequencies, and age of acquisition. The model achieved the state-of-the-art results for English datasets during the CWI Shared Task 2018 (Yimam et al., 2018), but the limitation of this approach is that it is hard to port from one language to another.

Kajiwara and Komachi (2018) developed a system for multilingual and cross-lingual CWI. The system was implemented using word frequencies features extracted from the learner corpus (Lang-8 corpus) Mizumoto et al. (2011), Wikipedia and WikiNews. The features contained the number of characters, the number of words, and the frequency of the target word. The system achieved state-of-the-art results for both Spanish and German datasets.

Aroyehun et al. (2018) developed systems for both English and Spanish using binary classification and deep learning (CNN) approaches. The feature-based approach used features such as word frequency of the target word from Wikipedia and Simple Wikipedia corpus, syntactic and lexical features, psycholinguistic features and entity features, and word embedding distance as a feature which is computed between the target word and the sentence. The deep learning approach used GloVe word embeddings (Pennington et al., 2014) to represent target words and its context. The deep learning approach is very simple and achieves better results than other deep learning approaches.

Our methodology follows that of Aroyehun et al. (2018) deep learning model in combination with word embeddings and linguistic features.

3   Model

In this section, we explain our approach based on Convolutional Neural Networks (CNN) trained on word embeddings and engineered features. Section 3.2 describes the details on how to preprocess data, transforming from a raw sentence into a matrix of numbers containing all the features described in Section 3.1. Section 3.3 describes the overall architecture of our network, Hyperparameters tuning and training details.

3.1   Features

In this section, we describe all features incorporated in our system.

Word Embeddings Feature: We use pre-trained word embeddings GloVe (Pennington et al., 2014) with 300 dimensions to extract word vector representation of each word for all the three languages. For English, we use the model trained on Wikipedia 2014 and Gigaword 5 model (6B tokens, 400K vocab).[1] For Spanish, we use the model (Cardellino, 2016) trained on 1.5 billion words data from different sources: dumps from the Spanish Wikipedia, Wikisource, and Wikibooks on date 2015-09-01, Spanish portion of SenSem, Spanish portion of Ancora Corpus, Tibidabo Treebank and IULA Spanish LSP Treebank, Spanish portion of the OPUS project corpora, and Spanish portion of the Europarl.[2] For German, we use

---

[1] `https://nlp.stanford.edu/projects/glove`

[2] `https://github.com/dccuchile/spanish-word-embeddings`

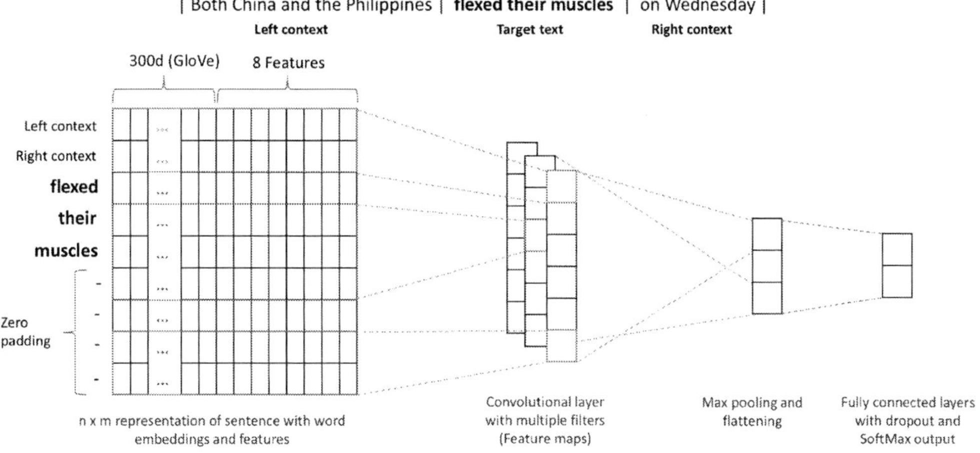

Figure 1: The model architecture

the model trained on the latest dumps of German Wikipedia.[3]

Morphological Features: Our morphological feature set consists of word frequency, word length, number of syllables, number of vowels, and tf-idf.

- Word frequency: the frequency of each word is extracted from the latest Wikipedia dumps as the raw count and then normalize to between 0 and 1.

- Word length: the number of character in the word.

- Number of syllables: the number of syllables of the word, calculated using Pyphen.[4]

- Number of vowels: the number of vowels in the word.

- tf-idf: Term frequency - inverse document frequency, calculated using scikit-learn library.[5]

Linguistic Features: The linguistic features consists of part-of-speech, dependency, and stop word.

- Part-of-speech (POS): a category to which a word is assigned in accordance with its syntactic functions, e.g. noun, pronoun, adjective, verb, etc.

- Dependency: a syntactic structure consists of relations between words, e.g. subject, preposition, verb, noun, adjective, etc.

- Stop word: a commonly used word such as "the", "a", "an", "in", "how", "what", "is", "you", etc.

All these features are extracted using SpaCy (Honnibal and Montani, 2017).

3.2 Preprocessing

We separate each sentence into three parts: target text, left context and right context. The target text is a word or a phrase which is selected and marked as complex or non-complex by the annotators. The left context and the right context are words that appear to the left and the right of the target text.

First, we remove all special characters, digits, and punctuation marks. Then, each word is replaced by its word vector representation using pre-trained word embeddings from the GloVe model as described in Section 3.1. Words that do not exist in the pre-trained word embeddings are replaced with zero vector. Afterward, we transform left context and right context into a 300-dimensional vector calculated as the average of the vectors of all the words in the left context and the right context. If left context or right context is empty (when the target text is at the beginning or the end of the sentence), we replace it with a zero vector. Next, we initialize a matrix X of size $n * m (n = h + 2, m = 308)$ where the first row corresponds to the left context vector, the second

---

[3]https://deepset.ai/
german-word-embeddings
[4]https://pyphen.org
[5]https://scikit-learn.org

row corresponds to the right context vector, and the last r rows are given by the embedding vectors of the words contained in the target text, where r is the number of words in the target text. In order to have a fixed size matrix, we pad the remaining rows p with zero vectors, where $p = h - r$ and h is the maximum value of r in the corpus.

To convert each feature into a vector representation, first we need to transform its values. For example:

- Part-of-speech and Dependency have values such as N, V, ADJ, ADV, and PREP, so we index as 1, 2, 3, 4, 5 and normalize it to between 0 and 1.

- Stop word: 1-stop word, 0-otherwise.

- All the values of word frequency, word length, number of syllables, number of vowels, and tf-idf are numbers, so we just normalize it to between 0 and 1.

For each feature, we initialize a matrix of one column and n rows where the first row corresponds to the average value of the left context, the second row corresponds to the average value of the right context, and the last r rows are the values of the feature for each word in the target text, and the remaining rows are padded with zero. Then, we append this matrix to the previous matrix X.

3.3 Hyperparameters and Training

Figure 1 shows the general architecture of our network. The model has been constructed using pure Tensorflow deep learning library version 1.14.[6]

We train our model using CNN with the number of filters 128, stride of 1, and kernel size of 3, 4, and 5. We then apply the ReLu activation function with Max Pooling to the out of this layer; the output of this layer is often called feature maps. The feature maps are flattened and pass through three Fully-Connected layers (FC) with dropout between each layer. The first two FC layers use ReLu activation function with 256 and 64 of outputs. The last FC layer uses Softmax activation function which provides the output as complex (1) or non-complex (0).

For all datasets, the training is done through Stochastic Gradient Descent over shuffle mini-batches using Adam optimizer (Kingma and Ba, 2014) with the learning rate of 0.001, dropout rate

of 0.25, mini-batch size of 128. Also, we use weighted cross-entropy as a loss function with the weight of 1.5 for the positive since our datasets are imbalanced; it contains roughly 60% negative examples and 40% positive examples as you can see in the Table 1. We train the system for 200 epochs, and for every 20 iterations, we validate the system with the shuffle development set. Then, if the model achieves the highest f1-score, we save the model and use it for our final evaluation with the test set. In our case, all the hyperparameters are selected via a grid search over the English development set.

We train and evaluate each language separately. For English, the dataset has three different genres, so we combine and train all at once. For Spanish and German, it has only one genre, so we use it directly for training.

4 Datasets

Table 1 shows all the details about each dataset used in the experiments.

Dataset	Train	Dev	Test	Positive
News	14,002	1,764	2,095	40%
WikiNews	7,746	870	1,287	42%
Wikipedia	5,551	694	870	45%
Spanish	13,750	1,622	2,233	40%
German	6,151	795	959	42%

Table 1: English, Spanish and German datasets

We use the CWIG3G2 datasets from (Yimam et al., 2017a,b) for our CWI system for both training and evaluation. The datasets are collected for multiple languages (English, Spanish, German). The English dataset contains news from three different genres: professionally written news, WikiNews (news written by amateurs), and Wikipedia articles. For Spanish and German, they are collected from Spanish and German Wikipedia articles. For English, each sentence is annotated by 10 native and 10 non-native speakers. For Spanish, it is mostly annotated by native speakers, whereas German it is annotated by more non-native than native speakers. Each sentence contains a target text which is selected by annotators, and it is marked as complex if at least one annotator annotates as complex.

---

[6]https://www.tensorflow.org

System	English			Spanish	German
	News	WikiNews	Wikipedia		
Camb (Gooding and Kochmar, 2018)	**87.36**	**84**	**81.15**	-	-
TMU (Kajiwara and Komachi, 2018)	86.32	78.73	76.19	76.99	74.51
NLP-CIC (Aroyehun et al., 2018)	85.51	83.08	77.2	76.72	
ITEC (De Hertog and Tack, 2018)	86.43	81.10	78.15	76.37	-
NILC (Hartmann and Santos, 2018)	86.36	82.77	79.65	-	-
CFILT_IITB (Wani et al., 2018)	84.78	81.61	77.57	-	-
SB@GU (Alfter, 2018)	83.25	80.31	78.32	72.81	69.92
Gillin Inc.	82.43	70.83	66.04	68.04	55.48
hu-berlin (Popović, 2018)	82.63	76.56	74.45	70.80	69.29
UnibucKernel (Butnaru and Ionescu, 2018)	81.78	81.27	79.19	-	-
LaSTUS/TALN (AbuRa'ed and Saggion, 2018)	81.03	74.91	74.02	-	-
Our CWI	86.79	83.86	80.11	**79.70**	**75.89**

Table 2: The evaluation results

5 Results

Table 2 shows the results of our model against others (all the results are based on macro-averaged F1-score).

Our evaluation has shown that when training with the dataset which has more training examples, the model achieves the better result. For example, the model achieves the score of 86.79 on the English News dataset with 14,002 examples compared to the score of 83.86 on the English WikiNews dataset with 7,746 examples and the score of 80.11 on the English Wikipedia dataset with 5,551 examples.

We have found an interesting problem. A word can be both complex and non-complex in the same sentence, depending on the selection of the target text. Consider the following sentence, for example,

> The distance, chemical composition, and age of Teide 1 could be established because of its membership in the young Pleiades star cluster.

- The target text "**Pleiades**" is annotated by 3 native and 2 non-native speakers as complex, and our system also predicts it as complex.

- The same sentence with different target text "**Pleiades star cluster**". None of native and non-native speakers annotate it as complex, but our system predicts it as complex.

Here is another example,

> Definitions have been determined such that the 'super casino' will have a minimum customer area of 5000 square metres and at most 1250 unlimited-jackpot slot machines.

- For the target text "**casino**", none of native and non-native speakers annotate it as complex, and our system also predicts it as non-complex.

- The same sentence with different target text "**super casino**". Only one non-native speaker annotates it as complex, so it is marked as complex, but our system predicts it as non-complex.

6 Conclusion and Future Work

In this paper, we have presented a new CWI approach that utilizes deep learning model (CNN) with word embeddings and engineered features. The evaluation has shown that our model performs quite well compared to the state-of-the-art system for English, which realizes on feature-engineered, and better than the state-of-the-art systems for both Spanish and German.

In future work, we plan to use deep contextualized word representations such as BERT (Devlin et al., 2018) or XLNet (Yang et al., 2019) instead of GloVe. Also, we plan to add more features which will be extracted from MRC psycholinguistics database (Paetzold and Specia, 2016a) such as age of acquisition, familarity, concretness, and imagery.

Acknowledgments

I would like to give special thanks to my supervisor, Prof. Horacio Saggion, for the advice, feedback, and suggestions. Also, I would like to thank the anonymous reviewers for their constructive comments.

References

Ahmed AbuRa'ed and Horacio Saggion. 2018. LaS-TUS/TALN at Complex Word Identification (CWI) 2018 Shared Task. *Proceedings of the Thirteenth Workshop on Innovative Use of NLP for Building Educational Applications* pages 159–165. https://doi.org/10.18653/v1/w18-0517.

David Alfter. 2018. SB @ GU at the Complex Word Identification 2018 Shared Task. *Proceedings of the Thirteenth Workshop on Innovative Use of NLP for Building Educational Applications* pages 315–321.

Segun Taofeek Aroyehun, Jason Angel, Daniel Alejandro Pérez Alvarez, and Alexander Gelbukh. 2018. Complex Word Identification: Convolutional Neural Network vs. Feature Engineering. *Proceedings of the Thirteenth Workshop on Innovative Use of NLP for Building Educational Applications* pages 322–327. https://doi.org/10.18653/v1/w18-0538.

Delphine Bernhard, Louis De Viron, Véronique Moriceau, and Xavier Tannier. 2012. Question generation for french: collating parsers and paraphrasing questions. *Dialogue & Discourse* 3(2):43–74.

Stefan Bott, Luz Rello, Biljana Drndarevic, and Horacio Saggion. 2012. Can Spanish be simpler? Lex-SiS: Lexical simplification for Spanish. In *Proceedings of COLING 2012*. Mumbai, India, pages 357–374.

Andrei M Butnaru and Radu Tudor Ionescu. 2018. UnibucKernel : A kernel-based learning method for complex word identification. *Proceedings ofthe Thirteenth Workshop on Innovative Use ofNLP for Building Educational Applications* pages 175–183.

Cristian Cardellino. 2016. Spanish Billion Words Corpus and Embeddings. https://crscardellino.github.io/SBWCE/.

R Chandrasekar, Christine Doran, and B Srinivas. 1996. Motivations and Methods of Text Simplification. In *Proceedings of the 16th conference on Computational linguistics-Volume 2*. 9, pages 1041–1044. https://www.aclweb.org/anthology/C96-2183 http://portal.acm.org/citation.cfm?id=993361.

Dirk De Hertog and Anaïs Tack. 2018. Deep Learning Architecture for Complex Word Identification. *Proceedings of the Thirteenth Workshop on Innovative Use of NLP for Building Educational Applications* pages 328–334. https://doi.org/10.18653/v1/w18-0539.

Jacob Devlin, Ming-Wei Chang, Kenton Lee, and Kristina Toutanova. 2018. Bert: Pre-training of deep bidirectional transformers for language understanding. *arXiv preprint arXiv:1810.04805* .

Richard J. Evans. 2011. Comparing methods for the syntactic simplification of sentences in information extraction. *Literary and Linguistic Computing* 26(4):371–388. https://doi.org/10.1093/llc/fqr034.

Sian Gooding and Ekaterina Kochmar. 2018. Camb at cwi shared task 2018: Complex word identification with ensemble-based voting. In *Proceedings of the Thirteenth Workshop on Innovative Use of NLP for Building Educational Applications*. pages 184–194.

Nathan Hartmann and Leandro Borges Santos. 2018. NILC at CWI 2018: Exploring Feature Engineering and Feature Learning. *Proceedings of the Thirteenth Workshop on Innovative Use of NLP for Building Educational Applications* pages 335–340. https://doi.org/10.18653/v1/w18-0540.

Matthew Honnibal and Ines Montani. 2017. spaCy 2: Natural language understanding with Bloom embeddings, convolutional neural networks and incremental parsing. To appear.

Siddhartha Jonnalagadda and Graciela Gonzalez. 2010. Sentence simplification aids protein-protein interaction extraction. *arXiv preprint arXiv:1001.4273* .

Tomoyuki Kajiwara and Mamoru Komachi. 2018. Complex Word Identification Based on Frequency in a Learner Corpus. *Proceedings of the Thirteenth Workshop on Innovative Use of NLP for Building Educational Applications* pages 195–199. https://doi.org/10.18653/v1/W18-0521.

Diederik P. Kingma and Jimmy Ba. 2014. Adam: A Method for Stochastic Optimization. *arXiv e-prints* page 103. https://doi.org/10.1145/1830483.1830503.

Gondy Leroy, James E Endicott, David Kauchak, Obay Mouradi, and Melissa Just. 2013. User evaluation of the effects of a text simplification algorithm using term familiarity on perception, understanding, learning, and information retention. *Journal of medical Internet research* 15(7):e144. https://doi.org/10.2196/jmir.2569.

Tomoya Mizumoto, Mamoru Komachi, Masaaki Nagata, and Yuji Matsumoto. 2011. Mining revision log of language learning sns for automated japanese error correction of second language learners. In *Proceedings of 5th International Joint Conference on Natural Language Processing*. pages 147–155.

Gustavo Paetzold and Lucia Specia. 2015. LEXenstein: A Framework for Lexical Simplification. In *Proceedings of ACL-IJCNLP 2015 System Demonstrations*. Association for Computational Linguistics and The Asian Federation of Natural Language Processing, Stroudsburg, PA, USA, pages 85–90. https://doi.org/10.3115/v1/P15-4015.

Gustavo Paetzold and Lucia Specia. 2016a. Inferring psycholinguistic properties of words. In *Proceedings of the 2016 Conference of the North American Chapter of the Association for Computational*

Linguistics: Human Language Technologies. pages 435–440.

Gustavo Paetzold and Lucia Specia. 2016b. Semeval 2016 task 11: Complex word identification. In *Proceedings of the 10th International Workshop on Semantic Evaluation (SemEval-2016).* pages 560–569.

Jeffrey Pennington, Richard Socher, and Christopher D. Manning. 2014. Glove: Global vectors for word representation. In *Empirical Methods in Natural Language Processing (EMNLP).* pages 1532–1543. http://www.aclweb.org/anthology/D14-1162.

Maja Popović. 2018. Complex word identification using character n-grams. In *Proceedings of the Thirteenth Workshop on Innovative Use of NLP for Building Educational Applications.* pages 341–348.

Horacio Saggion. 2017. Automatic Text Simplification. *Synthesis Lectures on Human Language Technologies* 10(1):1–137.

Horacio Saggion, Sanja Štajner, Stefan Bott, Simon Mille, Luz Rello, and Biljana Drndarevic. 2015. Making It Simplext. *ACM Transactions on Accessible Computing* 6(4):1–36. https://doi.org/10.1145/2738046.

Advaith Siddharthan. 2002. An architecture for a text simplification system. In *Language Engineering Conference, 2002. Proceedings.* IEEE, pages 64–71.

Advaith Siddharthan, Ani Nenkova, and Kathleen McKeown. 2004. Syntactic simplification for improving content selection in multi-document summarization. In *Proceedings of the 20th international conference on Computational Linguistics.* Association for Computational Linguistics, page 896.

Sanja Štajner and Maja Popovic. 2016. Can Text Simplification Help Machine Translation? *In Proceedings of the 19th Annual Conference of the European Association for Machine Translation* 4(2):230–242.

Nikhil Wani, Sandeep Mathias, Jayashree Aanand Gajjam, and Pushpak Bhattacharyya. 2018. The Whole is Greater than the Sum of its Parts : Towards the Effectiveness of Voting Ensemble Classifiers for Complex Word Identification. *Proceedings of the Thirteenth Workshop on Innovative Use of NLP for Building Educational Applications* pages 200–205.

Willian Massami Watanabe, Arnaldo Candido Junior, Vinícius Rodrigues de Uzêda, Renata Pontin de Mattos Fortes, Thiago Alexandre Salgueiro Pardo, and Sandra Maria Aluísio. 2009. Facilita: Reading Assistance for Low-literacy Readers Willian. *Proceedings of the 2010 International Cross Disciplinary Conference on Web Accessibility (W4A) - W4A '10* page 1. https://doi.org/10.1145/1805986.1805997.

Zhilin Yang, Zihang Dai, Yiming Yang, Jaime Carbonell, Ruslan Salakhutdinov, and Quoc V Le. 2019. Xlnet: Generalized autoregressive pretraining for language understanding. *arXiv preprint arXiv:1906.08237 .*

Seid Muhie Yimam, Chris Biemann, Shervin Malmasi, Gustavo H Paetzold, Lucia Specia, Sanja Štajner, Anaïs Tack, and Marcos Zampieri. 2018. A report on the complex word identification shared task 2018. *arXiv preprint arXiv:1804.09132 .*

Seid Muhie Yimam, Sanja Štajner, Martin Riedl, and Chris Biemann. 2017a. Cwig3g2-complex word identification task across three text genres and two user groups. In *Proceedings of the Eighth International Joint Conference on Natural Language Processing (Volume 2: Short Papers).* pages 401–407.

Seid Muhie Yimam, Sanja Štajner, Martin Riedl, and Chris Biemann. 2017b. Multilingual and Cross-Lingual ComplexWord Identification. In *RANLP 2017 - Recent Advances in Natural Language Processing Meet Deep Learning.* Incoma Ltd. Shoumen, Bulgaria, pages 813–822. http://www.acl-bg.org/proceedings/2017/RANLP 2017/pdf/RANLP104.pdf.

Neural Network-Based Models with Commonsense Knowledge for Machine Reading Comprehension

Denis Smirnov

National Research University Higher School of Economics

Moscow, Russia

dmsmirnov@hse.ru

Abstract

State-of-the-art machine reading comprehension models are capable of producing answers for factual questions about a given piece of text. However, some type of questions requires commonsense knowledge which cannot be inferred from the given text passage. Thus, external semantic information could enhance the performance of these models. This PhD research proposal provides a brief overview of some existing machine reading comprehension datasets and models and outlines possible ways of their improvement.

1 Introduction

Machine reading comprehension (MRC) is one of the well-studied problems in artificial intelligence. This problem can be defined as a problem of creating an algorithm, which can understand the content of a given text in natural language, which is used by humans to communicate with each other. There is no formal way to define the quality of understanding. One of the most popular approaches to measure the understanding is the assess the ability to answer the questions about the given text, hence the problem of machine reading comprehension is closely related to the question answering problem and these concepts are often used as synonyms.

Question answering is a vital component of many real-world systems. More accurate answers to questions on the text, will improve the performance of intelligent assistants and search engines on the Internet or corporate knowledge bases.

There exist many datasets used to assess question answering models which contain texts and questions about its contents. This could be either multiple choice questions (Richardson, 2013),

cloze-style questions, which require filling in the gap in the question definition (Hermann et al., 2015) or open questions, where the answer is a named entity from the context (Rajpurkar et al., 2018).

State-of-the-art question answering models perform fairly well for factual questions when the answer is clearly stated in the text but they fail to achieve comparable performance on questions which require common sense inference. This type of questions is often simple for humans but can be challenging for an algorithm because an answer cannot be derived without external knowledge about semantic relationships of entities described in the given text. Examples of such questions are demonstrated in the next section.

2 QA Datasets that Require Commonsense Knowledge

A well-known problem for commonsense evaluation is the Winograd Schema Challenge (WSC) (Levesque, 2011). The schema of the text passages and questions is based on co-reference resolution. The first part of the text mentions two entities, while the second part contains a pronoun or a possessive adjective which refer to any of the introduced entities. To illustrate the problem, consider the following question from the WSC dataset:

> Sam pulled up a chair to the piano, but it was broken, so he had to stand instead.
> What was broken?
> - The chair *(correct answer)*
> - The piano

The original dataset for the problem is very small, it contains only 150 schemas, as the new samples must be thoroughly handcrafted by humans. The most recent version consists of 285

Proceedings of the Student Research Workshop associated with RANLP-2019, pages 90–94,
Varna, Bulgaria, Sep 2–4, 2019.
https://doi.org/10.26615/issn.2603-2821.2019_014

schemas. This task remains difficult for models, state-of-the-art approach reports only 71.06% success rate for the problem (Prakash et al., 2019).

A more recent dataset for machine reading comprehension with commonsense knowledge is MCScript (Ostermann et al., 2018). It contains around 2100 scripts (narrative texts describing everyday activities) and approx. 14000 questions, written by crowdsourced workers Authors estimate that commonsense reasoning is required to answer 27.4% of questions.

More large-scale dataset was introduced by Zhang et al. (2018). Authors designed a multistage procedure to generate passage-question-answer triplets from CNN/Daily Mail dataset and Internet Archive which included performed automatic filtering of the triplets, leaving only those, which were unanswerable by the competitive MRC model, and further manual human filtering resulting in 120000 cloze-form questions. Authors analyzed a sample of resulting passages and questions and concluded, that automatic filtering allowed to exclude most of the questions, which could be answered with paraphrasing, while human filtering excluded ambiguous questions. 75% of sampled questions required commonsense reasoning or multisentence inference to obtain an answer.

A scalable approach for commonsence question generation and a new dataset, which consists from more than 12000 multiple-choice questions, was recently introduced by Talmor et al. (2019). In this dataset, questions are based on extracted subgraphs from ConceptNet. Given an extracted source concept and three target concepts, connected with the source by the same relation, crowdsourcers were asked to write three questions, that contain source concept and have only one of the target concepts as an answer. At the next stage, two more answer choices are added, to make the problem more challenging.

Below is an example question from CommonsenseQA:

> Where would I not want a fox?
> - hen house *(correct answer)*
> - england
> - mountains
> - english hunt
> - california

Authors also performed multiple experimental evaluations and showed, that current state-of-the-art models are far away from human performance on this dataset.

3 Existing Approaches

Modern approaches to question answering problem mostly rely on deep neural networks. More specifically, they often use recurrent neural networks (RNNs), a special type of networks, which process input sequentially. In such networks, the result of the processing of previous input affects the consecutive outputs. One limitation of this architecture is that the state is updated on each timestep, so it is hard to keep track of long-range dependencies. This happens because of the vanishing gradient problem. To address this issue a modification of recurrent layer called Long Short-Term Memory (LSTM) was introduced (Hochreiter and Schmidhuber, 1997). In this type of layer, there is an additional path to carry data flow (carry flow) through time steps, which is capable of capturing long-range dependencies. Another possible improvement of RNN architecture, frequently used in NLP models, is the simultaneous processing of input sequence in s forward and backward direction, which is done in bi-directional RNNs (Schuster and Paliwal, 1997). The same trick can be applied to LSTM (BiLSTM) (Graves and Schmidhuber, 2005).

A standard component of deep neural networks in the whole natural language processing domain are embeddings. They are used to transform words into low-dimensional dense real-valued vector representation which can be easily used as an input for any type of neural network. There are several standard embeddings pre-trained on large text corpora, like Word2Vec (Mikolov et al., 2013), GloVe (Pennington et al., 2014), or FastText (Bojanowski et al., 2017), and most of the question answering models use one of the available implementations.

The rest of this section describes several architectures of the most important approaches for question answering problem. The architectures under consideration both use and do not use the external semantic information.

3.1 RNN-Based Models

BiDAF (Bi-Directional Attention Flow) was proposed by Seo et al. (2017). In this architecture, embeddings are calculated using the input data (pair context and question) both at the word level and at the character level (using the convolutional network char-CNN). Embeddings vectors are fed as an input to BiLSTM, the context and the question use layers that are not interconnected. Then, the attention mechanism is applied to the activations of these layers (it is proposed to use it in two directions from the context to the question and vice versa) and the result passes through one common two-layer BiLSTM and the final layer forms the answer.

One notable model for machine reading comprehension is DAANet (Xiao et al., 2018). This architecture does not use any external semantic information. However, the dual learning objective of this model deserves attention. Instead of training the model with a single task to answer the question, the authors proposed a way to simultaneously train the network to generate a question using the answer and generate the answer using the question.

3.2 Pre-Trained Language Models

Nowadays, the best results in many datasets are achieved by universal deep pre-trained language models that are fine-tuned for a specific task.

The common limitation of the models, which use Word2Vec, GloVe, FasText or similar embeddings is the static nature of word vectors obtained by such embeddings. The word vector values are the same, regardless of the context, and thus, these embeddings are not capable of capturing polysemy. At the same time, embeddings, obtained with language models, overcome this issue, they produce different vectors for words in different contexts.

One of the best models in this category is Bidirectional Encoder Representations from Transformers (BERT) (Devlin et al., 2019). The main innovation of this model is the training method, in which, unlike the usual approach to learning language models (when the objective is to predict the next word), the network learned to predict a randomly chosen masked word in a phrase and thus learned the representation of the surrounding context of the word.

Another deep language model also based on transformer architecture (Vaswani et al., 2017) is GPT-2 (Radford et al., 2019). While BERT was originally trained on BooksCorpus and English Wikipedia, GPT-2 was trained on a more diverse set of Internet texts. It also has much more trainable parameters (1.5B in the largest unreleased version vs. 340M in the BERT-large). Authors claim that GPT-2 achieves state-of-the-art results on several NLP tasks, including the Winograd Schema Challenge.

3.3 Adding Commonsense to Models

When it comes to enrichment of models with commonsense knowledge, semantic networks are the number one choice. One of the largest semantic networks is ConceptNet (Speer et al., 2017), where one can find a vocabularies of concepts in multiple languages, which are interconnected by 34 relations, forming a graph with 34 million edges.

A few attempts to add external semantic information are found in the works of Wang et al. (2018) and González et al. (2018). which use information from ConceptNet. Wang et al. (2018) propose the model, which is similar to BiDAF with the only exception that the embeddings of words and features from context, question and answer are also considered, then they pass through separate BiLSTM layers and their activations are aggregated with attention. In the features of the model, which are counted for context, there is a place for a vector of 10 values, encoding the relation of a word and any of the words in a question or answer (the fact that there is an edge in ConceptNet). If there are several such relations, one is chosen randomly.

An approach of González et al. (2018) is the replacement of standard embeddings with NumberBatch semantic vectors, trained using connections from ConceptNet. As far as embeddings are a standard component of deep neural networks in natural language processing domain, this approach of embeddings replacement allows enriching a great variety of neural network-based models with external semantic information, contained in word representation.

The missing knowledge can be extracted not only from knowledge graphs, but also from the text repositories. One possible technique is the knowledge hunting. In case of co-reference resolution problem like in WSC, knowledge hunting would consist in finding the similar piece of text, which does not have ambiguity in referencing mentioned entities. This method have been successfully applied to WSC by Prakash et al. (2019). Authors combined a two-stage knowledge hunting procedure with the outputs of a neural language model using a probabilistic soft logic, and it currently achieves state-of-the art results in this challenge.

4 Discussion

We have seen so far, that even enormous pre-trained deep language models cannot pick up the ability to reason about the text, even when trained on large and diverse corpora, so the improvement of methods of extraction and representation of commonsense knowledge in neural networks is one of the directions of my PhD research.

The idea from DAANet (Xiao et al., 2018) could be used in a modified version of such model, which can simultaneously produce a query to a semantic network (i.e question about the text) and an answer to a given target question. This approach could be a possible solution to the problem of defining relevant external information for question answering algorithm.

The improvement of extraction and representation of commonsense knowledge is only one aspect of the work. So far we have explored the datasets and models for English language, which has enormous amount of labeled and unlabeled resources. Other languages have much less available resources for training. Another difficulty arises, when the same models are being applied to more agglutinative languages, which require morphological disambiguation, like Russian. The adaptation of existing models to Russian is another direction of my work.

Deep pre-trained language models can be trained in multilingual setting, and, for example, BERT nominally supports Russian. However, the monolingual model outperforms multilingual version (Devlin et al., 2019). It has been shown, that multilingual model can be a good initialization for finetuning of monolingual version of the model (Kuratov and Arkhipov, 2019). Exploration of the possibilities and limitations of transfer learning between languages for question answering.

Finally, the lack of resources for evaluation of models for Russian language, encourages me to collect my own dataset for machine reading comprehension.

Acknowledgments

I would like to express my appreciation to Dr. Dmitry Ilvovsky, my research supervisor, for his valuable and constructive suggestions during the planning and development of this work.

References

Piotr Bojanowski, Edouard Grave, Armand Joulin, and Tomas Mikolov. 2017. Enriching word vectors with subword information. *TACL* 5:135–146.

Jacob Devlin, Ming-Wei Chang, Kenton Lee, and Kristina Toutanova. 2019. BERT: Pre-training of deep bidirectional transformers for language understanding. In *Proceedings of the 2019 Conference of the North American Chapter of the Association for Computational Linguistics: Human Language Technologies, Volume 1 (Long and Short Papers)*. Association for Computational Linguistics, Minneapolis, Minnesota.

José-Ángel González, Lluís-F. Hurtado, Encarna Segarra, and Ferran Pla. 2018. ELiRF-UPV at SemEval-2018 task 11: Machine comprehension using commonsense knowledge. In *Proceedings of The 12th International Workshop on Semantic Evaluation*. Association for Computational Linguistics, New Orleans, Louisiana.

A. Graves and J. Schmidhuber. 2005. Framewise phoneme classification with bidirectional lstm networks. In *Proceedings. 2005 IEEE International Joint Conference on Neural Networks, 2005..* volume 4, pages 2047–2052 vol. 4.

Karl Moritz Hermann, Tomas Kocisky, Edward Grefenstette, Lasse Espeholt, Will Kay, Mustafa Suleyman, and Phil Blunsom. 2015. Teaching machines to read and comprehend. In C. Cortes, N. D. Lawrence, D. D. Lee, M. Sugiyama, and R. Garnett, editors, *Advances in Neural Information Processing Systems 28*, Curran Associates, Inc., pages 1693–1701.

Sepp Hochreiter and Jürgen Schmidhuber. 1997. Long short-term memory. *Neural Comput.* 9(8):1735–1780.

Yuri Kuratov and Mikhail Arkhipov. 2019. Adaptation of deep bidirectional multilingual transformers for russian language. *CoRR* abs/1905.07213.

Hector J. Levesque. 2011. The winograd schema challenge. In *Logical Formalizations of Commonsense Reasoning, Papers from the 2011 AAAI Spring Symposium, Technical Report SS-11-06, Stanford, California, USA, March 21-23, 2011*.

Tomas Mikolov, Ilya Sutskever, Kai Chen, Greg S Corrado, and Jeff Dean. 2013. Distributed representations of words and phrases and their compositionality. In C. J. C. Burges, L. Bottou, M. Welling, Z. Ghahramani, and K. Q. Weinberger, editors, *Advances in Neural Information Processing Systems 26*, Curran Associates, Inc., pages 3111–3119.

Simon Ostermann, Ashutosh Modi, Michael Roth, Stefan Thater, and Manfred Pinkal. 2018. MCScript: A Novel Dataset for Assessing Machine Comprehension Using Script Knowledge. In Nicoletta Calzolari (Conference chair), Khalid Choukri, Christopher Cieri, Thierry Declerck, Sara Goggi, Koiti Hasida, Hitoshi Isahara, Bente Maegaard, Joseph Mariani, Hlne Mazo, Asuncion Moreno, Jan Odijk, Stelios Piperidis, and Takenobu Tokunaga, editors, *Proceedings of the Eleventh International Conference on Language Resources and Evaluation (LREC 2018)*. European Language Resources Association (ELRA), Miyazaki, Japan.

Jeffrey Pennington, Richard Socher, and Christopher Manning. 2014. Glove: Global vectors for word representation. In *Proceedings of the 2014 Conference on Empirical Methods in Natural Language Processing (EMNLP)*. Association for Computational Linguistics, Doha, Qatar.

Ashok Prakash, Arpit Sharma, Arindam Mitra, and Chitta Baral. 2019. Combining knowledge hunting and neural language models to solve the Winograd schema challenge. In *Proceedings of the 57th Annual Meeting of the Association for Computational Linguistics*. Association for Computational Linguistics, Florence, Italy.

Alec Radford, Jeff Wu, Rewon Child, David Luan, Dario Amodei, and Ilya Sutskever. 2019. Language models are unsupervised multitask learners .

Pranav Rajpurkar, Robin Jia, and Percy Liang. 2018. Know what you don't know: Unanswerable questions for SQuAD. In *Proceedings of the 56th Annual Meeting of the Association for Computational Linguistics (Volume 2: Short Papers)*. Association for Computational Linguistics, Melbourne, Australia.

Matthew Richardson. 2013. Mctest: A challenge dataset for the open-domain machine comprehension of text. In *Proceedings of the 2013 Conference on Emprical Methods in Natural Language Processing (EMNLP 2013)*.

M. Schuster and K. K. Paliwal. 1997. Bidirectional recurrent neural networks. *IEEE Transactions on Signal Processing* 45(11):2673–2681.

Min Joon Sco, Aniruddha Kembhavi, Ali Farhadi, and Hannaneh Hajishirzi. 2017. Bidirectional attention flow for machine comprehension. In *5th International Conference on Learning Representations, ICLR 2017, Toulon, France, April 24-26, 2017, Conference Track Proceedings*.

Robyn Speer, Joshua Chin, and Catherine Havasi. 2017. Conceptnet 5.5: An open multilingual graph of general knowledge. In *Proceedings of the Thirty-First AAAI Conference on Artificial Intelligence, February 4-9, 2017, San Francisco, California, USA.*. pages 4444–4451.

Alon Talmor, Jonathan Herzig, Nicholas Lourie, and Jonathan Berant. 2019. CommonsenseQA: A question answering challenge targeting commonsense knowledge. In *Proceedings of the 2019 Conference of the North American Chapter of the Association for Computational Linguistics: Human Language Technologies, Volume 1 (Long and Short Papers)*. Association for Computational Linguistics, Minneapolis, Minnesota.

Ashish Vaswani, Noam Shazeer, Niki Parmar, Jakob Uszkoreit, Llion Jones, Aidan N Gomez, Ł ukasz Kaiser, and Illia Polosukhin. 2017. Attention is all you need. In I. Guyon, U. V. Luxburg, S. Bengio, H. Wallach, R. Fergus, S. Vishwanathan, and R. Garnett, editors, *Advances in Neural Information Processing Systems 30*, Curran Associates, Inc., pages 5998–6008.

Liang Wang, Meng Sun, Wei Zhao, Kewei Shen, and Jingming Liu. 2018. Yuanfudao at SemEval-2018 task 11: Three-way attention and relational knowledge for commonsense machine comprehension. In *Proceedings of The 12th International Workshop on Semantic Evaluation*. Association for Computational Linguistics, New Orleans, Louisiana.

Hang Xiao, Feng Wang, Jianfeng Yan, and Jingyao Zheng. 2018. Dual ask-answer network for machine reading comprehension. *CoRR* abs/1809.01997.

Sheng Zhang, Xiaodong Liu, Jingjing Liu, Jianfeng Gao, Kevin Duh, and Benjamin Van Durme. 2018. Record: Bridging the gap between human and machine commonsense reading comprehension. *CoRR* abs/1810.12885.

Author Index

Association for Computational Linguistics
209 N. Eighth Street
Stroudsburg, Pennsylvania 18360

ISBN 978-1-7138-0296-9